felt

felt

IRRESISTIBLY BEAUTIFUL PROJECTS

Robyn Steel-Stickland

St. Martin's Griffin
New York

www.stmartins.com

Illustrations copyright © 2006 by Penguin Group (Australia).
Photography copyright © 2006 by Penguin Group (Australia).
Design by Claire Tice © 2006 Penguin Group (Australia).
Illustrations by Tracie Grimwood
Photography by Julie Anne Renouf

Library of Congress Cataloging-in-Publication Data Available Upon Request

ISBN-13: 978-0-312-36058-0
ISBN-10: 0-312-36058-4

First published in Australia by Penguin Group (Australia), a division of Pearson Australia Group Pty Ltd, 2006

First U.S. Edition: October 2006

10 9 8 7 6 5 4 3 2 1

contents

the magic of felt

Felt is like no other textile medium, and to make felt you don't need to be a great artist. You don't even need to know how to sew or to draw. You simply need to open your imagination and experiment, and soon you'll be able to create beautiful textiles for your home.

You can use a range of suitable materials in a variety of ways, and reconstruct them to create your own unique piece of fabric. What could be more exciting or full of creative possibility than that? The emphasis of this book is on looking at the surface of the felt and exploring all the wonderful things you can do to alter it and make it your own. Felt is incredibly versatile. It is strong and warm, can be as fine as gossamer, or as chunky as a thick woolen sweater. You can enrich and embellish the surface as much or as little as you choose.

I hope this book will inspire you. Clear step-by-step instructions show how to undertake a series of projects that will have you working with wool fibers, water, soap and a little elbow grease to create your own textiles. Feltmaking isn't rocket science but it is a highly skilled art and craft form that has been practiced for thousands of years across many cultures.

It is important to remember that there are no hard and fast rules to the art of making felt. The end result will be affected by the amount of fleece that is laid out, by the addition of other fibers and fabrics, and by the amount of energy you use when rolling the felt. There are many happy accidents, and some things you will never repeat, but there is no 'wrong' way. Every felt maker works differently and has her preferred method. What follows is a guideline to the way I make felt, to set you on the path to your own adventure.

how to use this book

Read the following chapter on feltmaking as an introduction to the history of the craft, the principles of felting, and the materials and equipment you will need to undertake the projects included in this book.

Each of the following sections then introduces the basic techniques: flat felting, pre-felting and making nuno felt. There are several projects that use each of these techniques for you to explore. Use each project as a jumping-off point – copy it if you want to, to get yourself started, then change the colors, shapes and motifs to make the design uniquely yours.

Some of the terms used in feltmaking that may be unfamiliar are summarized in the glossary, and a series of felting tips is also included to help point you in the right direction if you are stuck. With feltmaking the emphasis is on fun and exploration, discovering the art anew every time you begin creating. Don't be afraid to break the rules – if it works for you, it works. To help you explore feltmaking further, a collection of felt resources will help you find books, classes, galleries and suppliers to develop your craft.

feltmaking

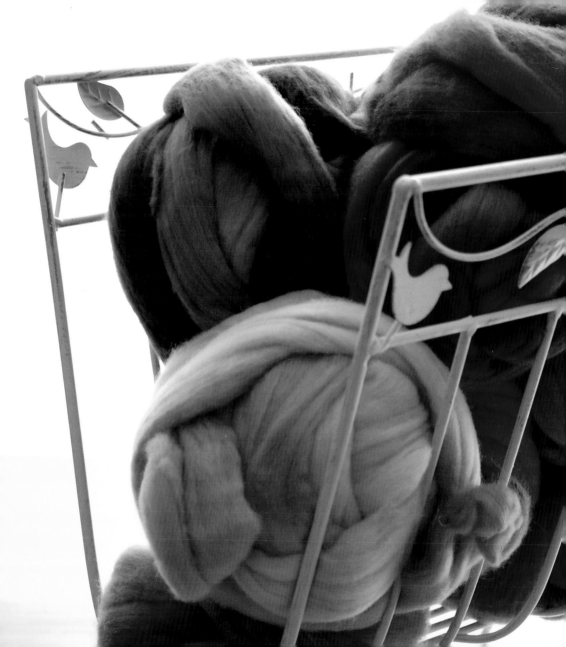

where does felt come from?

Felt is the oldest textile, dating back to the Bronze Age, with the oldest known artifact dating to the ninth century BC. Felt was made before people learned to spin, weave or knit, originating in Central Asia in a region extending from China and Mongolia through Kyrgyzstan to Turkey. The ancient nomadic shepherds are most likely to have been the first feltmakers, given that they lived and worked with sheep, which were among the first domesticated animals. It is possible that felt was originally made by accident, by lining a shoe or a place to sleep with plucked wool and then walking or sleeping on it for a few days, creating felt, which they eventually adapted for wearing in place of skins.

A range of ancient felts have been discovered, mostly preserved under freezing conditions in Siberian and Chinese tomb sites. They include articles of clothing such as shepherds' cloaks, boot linings, socks and stockings, felt caps, saddle covers and bags, carpets, yurts and wall coverings. Traditional felt, made in the same manner for hundreds of years, is still in use in the everyday lives of the people of Krygyzstan, Turkmenistan, Uzbekistan, Kazakhstan, and parts of Mongolia and China.

One of the most wonderful aspects of these ancient felts is that they are designed and constructed using very sophisticated techniques. Although these nomadic people had no written language, their felts are far from simple and naïve. On the contrary, these people were confident artists who used their materials with great skill. They used appliqué and inlay techniques that today we consider to be complex.

why does wool felt?

Felt is a non-woven fabric made of tangled wool fibers that have been wetted, agitated and matted together. It is the structure of the wool fiber that makes this possible. If you run your finger along a single wool fiber you will feel that in one direction it is smooth, and in the other it is rougher. The overlapping scales act like barbs on a fishing hook – they catch together and can't be separated. The fibers move in a worm-like action as they are agitated, curling around themselves and pulling up to the root end. One of the benefits of felt is that it can be cut without fraying.

Magnified wool fiber showing overlapping scales

There are several ways to make felt, but the projects in this book use wet felting techniques. There are also dry felting techniques such as needle-felting, which uses a barbed needle and can be done by hand or machine. A washing machine can also be used, but this method tends to over-felt the work; knitted felt is made in this way, and I think it's highly overrated because you are not in control. Electric sanding machines are also sometimes mentioned, but I'm not an advocate of using them because of the danger involved – electricity and water don't mix.

Hand-rolled felt has an entirely different quality from commercial machine-made felt. Apart from being warm and insulating, hand-rolled felt can also be soft and snuggly, or elegant and drapable. It can be used to make practical items or whimsical works of art, and along the way you can have an upper-body workout!

The quality of the felt you produce will be affected by many things, most notably the type of wool you use. The wool fibers vary according to the breed of sheep and the condition and length of its fleece. Wool fibers vary in length and diameter and are measured in microns. This is the term used in the wool trade, where a micron is the measure of the diameter of the wool fiber. Most wool fibers range from 2–12″ in length and from 14–45 microns in diameter. Merino wool is one on the finest breeds available and is easy to access. Polwarth is one of my personal favorites as it has a soft, fluffy quality when felted. Make samples using different breeds and qualities of wool so that you can make your own choice. Coarse wools are more appropriate for thick rugs and boots, while fine wools are better for wraps and scarves.

As a general rule the wool will shrink by 30–40 per cent as it felts. The shrinkage will be affected by how thickly or thinly the fleece is laid out, by how much you roll it, and by how far you full it. Heat and soap also contribute to this process, by encouraging the fibers to become swollen, making them more likely to move and entangle.

How to felt

To felt your piece you need to use a rolling technique, rolling the felt many times in order to agitate the fibers so that they will shrink and mat together. The felt will shrink in the direction that it is rolled, so if you want to keep the same shape you laid out, turn ninety degrees rather than rolling from end to end. Use a gentle rolling action, with your hands working along the length of the felting mat, working from fingertips to palm in a gentle rocking motion, applying pressure as you move your hands in and out along the mat.

equipment for feltmaking

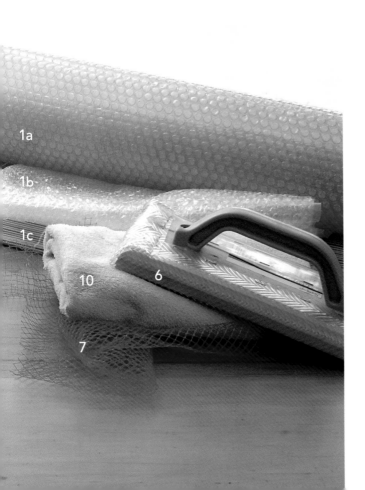

1 a Pool cover
1 b Plastic bubble wrap
1 c Matchstick blind

2   Plain nylon net
     curtaining

3   A sturdy plastic bottle
     with holes in the lid

4 a Dishwashing detergent
4 b Olive oil soap
4 c 'Sludge'

5   Plastic freezer bags

6   Wooden trowel /
     rubbing-in tool

7   Plastic mesh bag

8   Scale

9   Rubber bands

10   Old bath towels

11 a Hand carders
11 b Drum carder

equipment for feltmaking

One of the great things about making felt is that it requires no fancy or expensive equipment. The most valuable and hard-working component in the process will be yourself, so embark on a day of feltmaking well-rested and well-nourished, ready for a day of physical activity.

When I first started making felt it was a much less refined process, requiring buckets of hot soapy water, which meant that water splashed everywhere – except on the wool. The most suitable place to work was outside, with bare feet and pants rolled up or wearing rubber boots. Thank goodness there have been great leaps forward in process and technique. Feltmaking now requires much less water and you can work at your table with little or no splashing.

The following is a list of the equipment that I use and that you will need to make the projects in this book; also listed are some optional supplies you might find useful.

1. FELTING MAT

The following items can be used as a felting mat, but they also have their own special area of use depending on the project.

a. Pool cover – this is a plastic swimming pool cover with bubbles on one side and smooth on the other, which can be found at swimming pool suppliers. This is my preferred surface for laying out and rolling fleece as it is long lasting and firm for rolling in. I work on the smooth side because I find this is easiest when wetting down; working on the bubble side requires more water as it runs into the channels on the surface.

b. Plastic bubble wrap – commercial bubble wrap available from stationers and postal supply stores. Available in large quantities, this is used for very delicate pieces that need to be rubbed rather than rolled.

c. Matchstick blind – the traditional tool for rolling felts in Central Asia, and still widely used. Cedar matchstick blinds are a better investment than bamboo because they last longer and don't tend to splinter as much. They are often available in reasonable condition discarded at the curbside and are excellent for making cords, fulling the felt in the final stages, and especially when making large or thick pieces such as rugs.

2. PLAIN NYLON NET CURTAINING

This is to cover the dry fleece after it has been laid out. Its purpose is to hold the dry fleece in place and protect it from moving about while it is being wet down. It needs to be soft and have plenty of holes in it to let the water through. Never use a shower curtain, as it is designed to repel water, and really hard stiff net tulle can be hard to use too. I buy nylon curtain by the yard in the curtain department of a fabric store as it is cheap and very soft. You can also try looking in bargain bins and thrift shops. It is easier to manage with several smaller pieces of net than one large piece. If you only have one piece of net and it is smaller than your project, then work by wetting one area at a time.

3. A STURDY PLASTIC BOTTLE WITH HOLES IN THE LID

Laundry detergent bottles and heavy plastic milk bottles (quart size) are excellent, but soft drink bottles are useless as they melt if the water is too hot. This bottle is used to shake warm-to-hot, slightly soapy water over the net-covered fleece. Drill or poke several small holes in the lid so that you get an even flow of water and can control the amount you shake onto the fleece.

4. DISHWASHING DETERGENT, OLIVE OIL SOAP AND 'SLUDGE'

Soap has two purposes: it acts as a lubricant and it helps the wool to absorb the water. Feltmakers seem to have their own particular preference when it comes to which soap to use; some like to make up a thick slushy solution of soap flakes and water called 'sludge', while others prefer to use detergent or soap. I'm not too fussy as long as it's gentle on my hands, and I use both detergent and olive oil soap. Oil-based saponified soaps are better than bathroom soap.

a. Detergent – squeeze just a couple of drops into your water bottle and then top up with warm-to-hot water – I like mine hand-hot, especially in winter.

b. Soap – wet down your fleece with water only and glide the cake of soap across the surface of the wet net.

c. 'Sludge' solution – cover the base of an ice cream container with about an inch of soap flakes, add two cups of boiling water and dissolve. Fill to the top of the container with cold water and leave to set like jelly.

5. PLASTIC FREEZER BAGS

Used like a glove when wetting down the fleece. Put your hand inside and glide over the wet net as you rub the fleece in a circular motion. Plastic disposable gloves don't work nearly as well and plastic shopping bags are too big. The freezer bag is my bag of choice. Let it dry out over a tap and reuse it next time.

6. WOODEN TROWEL OR RUBBING-IN TOOL

I use mine to rub in wet pre-felted pieces to help them join together; I also use it like an iron at the end of the process to smooth out the damp felt. It's a wooden float or trowel from a hardware store with hard textured plastic covering its base.

7. PLASTIC MESH BAG

Use the type from supermarkets that contain oranges or onions. Cut open the empty bag to make one flat piece. Place this over the wet fleece after you have removed the net and before you use the trowel to rub in pre-felt pieces. It protects the fleece from being moved around while you rub the pre-felts into place. Make sure you remove the mesh after the pre-felts have been rubbed into place. If you leave the mesh on and keep rubbing then the fleece will start to felt to the mesh.

8. FINE PLASTIC DROP SHEET

Use a sheet slightly bigger than the project when it is wet down – or several small pieces. The purpose of a plastic drop sheet is to protect the wet fleece. Place it over the top of the wet fibers after you have removed the net, forming a sandwich with the wet fleece between the smooth side of the bubble wrap and the plastic sheet. Leave the plastic sheet in place while you are rolling the felt to keep embellishments from coming adrift or catching on the bubbles and being moved out of place.

9. SCALE

A small kitchen scale can be used to weigh the wool for a project – digital scales are the most accurate for small weights.

10. RUBBER BANDS

Use thick rubber bands or a piece of old elastic or stocking to hold the pool cover or bubble wrap rolled up.

11. AN ICE CREAM CONTAINER OR SMALL BUCKET

This can be kept near your work area to catch excess water squeezed from the felt, to hold hot water for dunking and reheating the felt, or for storing your materials.

12. OLD BATH TOWELS

Keep towels handy to mop up any spills or dribbles, and to lay flat on the table under the bubble wrap when rolling the felt — it stops the roll from slipping and soaks up the drips.

13. HAND CARDERS OR A DRUM CARDER

Optional and not necessary for these projects as they use carded fleece. This is the most expensive item you're likely to invest in and available from spinners' and weavers' groups and through large yarn shops. It is used to card un-carded or unprocessed fleece, or to mix colors by carding different shades together to enhance your palette.

14. SCISSORS, SEWING NEEDLES, PINS AND SEWING THREAD

These are used when working with pre-felts or to make occasional repairs or holding stitches when something isn't quite going right.

materials for feltmaking

In Australia we are immensely lucky to have the world's most beautiful wool at our fingertips. Merino is the finest and most commonly available wool for feltmaking; 'slivers' or 'tops' – ropes of loose unspun wool fibers that have been carded or sorted – are available pre-dyed or ready to be dyed. If there are no suppliers in your area don't despair as most of the businesses listed offer a mail order service (see page 131).

Most wool will felt. If it doesn't then it has probably been chemically treated and the chemical is prohibiting the process, or for some reason, such as age and storage conditions, the scales on the wool have started to break down, preventing the felting process from occurring. While there are only a few fibers that will actually felt – such as wool, alpaca, mohair and cashmere – there are countless other additional materials that can be trapped by the wool fibers to enhance the surface and create luscious textured felt.

The following list covers the materials I use when making felt, but don't be limited by my choices – try anything!

1. WOOL

Merino, Polwarth, Border Leicester, Romney and other sheep breeds, as well as mohair, alpaca, cashmere and more. Available as wool tops or slivers, wool batts (layered, carded sheets of wool), wool and pencil rovings (slivers of fiber prepared in long narrow strips), and waste from wool processing such as nops and scoured wool (fun for decorating the surface of the felt).

2. SILK

The most popular embellishment, silk is available in a variety of forms: silk tops, silk hankies, silk laps, silk throwster's waste, silk noils and more. The application of silk enhances the texture of the felt, creating beautiful shimmer and sheen.

silk

3. KNITTING YARN AND EMBROIDERY THREAD

Choose yarn with a high percentage of wool so that it will felt to the wool tops. Make the most of the knitting resurgence and enhance your felt with the fabulous variety of knitting yarns that are available. Knitting yarns and embroidery threads can be used to inlay patterns on the surface of the felt, to add decorative stitches, or to create loops and tassels.

embroidery thread

4. FABRIC

Choose fabrics with an open weave such as cotton, silk, cheesecloth and muslin; you can also use loosely woven synthetic fabrics, although these are more difficult to felt.

5. EMBELLISHMENTS

Nylon glitz (a bundle of glitzy fibers), chopped-up sewing threads, handmade paper, string, beads, flower heads and found objects. (In my experience feathers will not felt.)

embellishments

All of these embellishments, and more, can be trapped by the wool fibers to enrich the surface of your work.

While all this might sound confusing, don't be afraid to ask your supplier for advice and suggestions. As you work through the projects in this book, you will see how different materials are used.

preparation

First decide on your project, materials and colors. Work in an area with no drafts or breezes, ideally on a large table that is at work-bench height so you can stand and work comfortably.

Lay your chosen felting mat on your work surface – if using bubblewrap or pool-cover then place these bubble side down – you will lay out the project directly onto this surface.

care and storage of wool

Store wool tops in a sealed dry environment (such as sealed plastic storage boxes and bags) and out of direct sunlight. If wool is stored in direct sunlight it will sweat and become damp.

Protect your fleece and finished felt from moths, silverfish and other pests – they are silent villains, whose presence can go unnoticed until you take a wool wrap out of the cupboard and find it is full of holes. Take regular action using environmentally friendly moth-repelling ingredients. If you do find moth eggs and larvae in your felt and wool, they can be killed by freezing them for 48 hours, sealed in a polythene bag.

Take care to rinse all traces of soap from your finished article; if it is not thoroughly rinsed the soap will dry and may rot the fabric. Use a diluted solution of vinegar and water (half a cup of vinegar to a bucket of water) to remove all residual soap.

All woolen garments tend to pill – use a special wool comb designed to remove pilling from knitted garments to shave off the pills without damaging the felt.

Wash felt pieces gently by hand in tepid water with a suitable wool wash detergent. Take care not to rub – this could cause further shrinkage – and rinse thoroughly.

Learning to make flat felt is the first step into this wonderful art and craft form. Laying out the wool tops evenly and consistently is probably the hardest thing to master, but remember that anything worth doing takes time. Don't despair if your first piece has holes in it – just keep trying until laying out the wool tops evenly becomes second nature.

flat felt

cushion

The idea for this cushion is very simple and can be translated into other projects: change the colors and length and it becomes a scarf; make it larger and hang it on the wall and it becomes a wall hanging; make it long and narrow and display it on the table as a table runner. Work in a color scheme that fits with your home decor or wardrobe.

cushion

MATERIALS Merino wool tops in chocolate, blue, brown and cream (shown here from Treetops Color Harmonies and Yarn Barn).
QUANTITY 2¼ oz wool tops in total.
LAID-OUT SIZE 27½" x 27½". FINISHED SIZE 17½" x 17½".

Laying out

1 Work on the smooth side of the felting mat.

2 Gently pull a manageable length off the wool tops, then tease the wool apart in small tufts.

2

3 Lay these tufts side by side and row by row, slightly overlapping them as you go (the way roof tiles are laid).

4 Continue to lay out in this manner until you have reached the desired size of the first layer (27½" × 27½").

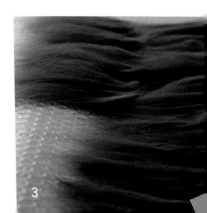

3

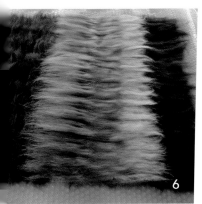

5 Lay out the first row of the second layer at right angles to the first layer. Use the same color as the bottom layer – I've used chocolate.

6 Continue to lay out, changing color with each row, until you have fully covered the first layer.

7 Repeat this with a third and final layer; three layers are suitable for a cushion.

8 Decorate the surface by splitting the wool tops off into fine pieces, then shape them into rings around your fingers and lay in place.

9 Repeat with smaller rings in a different color and nest them inside the larger rings.

10 When finished decorating the surface, carefully cover the laid-out wool tops with netting – taking care not to disturb the design which you have created underneath.

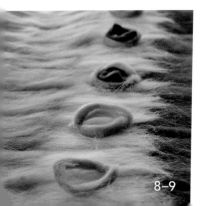

Wetting down the fleece

11 Fill a plastic bottle that has holes in the lid with warm water and a few drops of detergent. Carefully shake this mixture over your work to wet down the fleece.

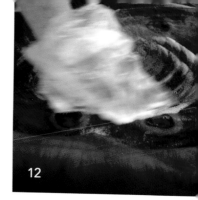

12 With your hand inside a plastic bag, rub the wetted area very gently in a circular motion. Work from the middle towards the edges to avoid moving the pieces around. *Work very slowly and gently* – you do not want to disturb what you've just laid out. Continue until the entire piece is flat and wet but not dripping – *dry areas will not felt*.

13 Very gently remove the net, lifting carefully at the corners and gently pulling away the wool that catches (it will catch because it starts to felt to the net if you rub too vigorously).

14 To keep areas of detail undisturbed while rolling, lay a fine plastic drop sheet over your work, and gently press the plastic into place.

15 Roll the piece up in the felting mat and place rubber bands around the ends of the roll to keep it secure.

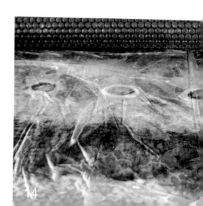

Rolling the felt

16 Lay a folded towel on the table and place the rolled felting mat on top of it – this is to soak up the drips and to stop the felting mat from slipping as you roll.

17 Roll the felting mat forward and backward 50 times, then unroll and check that the work hasn't moved (it's unlikely to have done so if covered with a sheet of plastic).

18 Gently reposition any pieces that have moved, then repeat the rolling and checking process three more times, turning the felt ninety degrees before re-rolling and rolling 50 times each time.

19 Repeat the rolling and checking process four more times, turning the felt ninety degrees each time and rolling 200 times each time. Reposition any pieces that have moved.

20 Unroll and gently fold the wool into a small parcel and squeeze out the water.

21 Reheat the felt by dipping it in hot water and squeezing out the excess.

22 Unfold the felt, reposition it on the felting mat, and roll up quickly to retain the heat.

23 Roll another 200 times, unroll and check. Repeat twice, re-rolling from the opposite end of the felting mat each time. You will see the wool starting to shrink up and go bubbly and lumpy like pebbles – this is good, it's what we want.

23

Fulling the felt

By now the felt should be strong enough to be 'thrown'. If you're not sure, roll another 200 times.

24 Fold the wet felt into a small parcel and squeeze out all the water.

25 Throw this parcel with all your might against a towel on your work table or on the floor. Refold it when it comes undone and repeat this throwing process about 20 times – you will see the felt begin to shrink rapidly.

26 Turn the felting mat to bubble side up. Unfold the wet felt and reposition it on the mat surface. If the felt is dry, sprinkle with warm soapy water.

27 Place your hands on the surface of the felt and gently manipulate it with a light pressure, moving the felt against the rough bubbles, using the surface like an old-fashioned washboard. This kneading process 'fulls' the felt causing rapid shrinkage as the bubbles act like a massager, gently moving the wool fibers against each other.

28 Continue to heat and manipulate the felt either by rolling or kneading until you have achieved the desired shrinkage and density.

29 To strengthen the edges of the felt roll them under your hand against the bubbles of the felting mat.

30 Rinse the felt with a solution of vinegar and water (half a cup of vinegar to a bucket of water) to remove the soap.

31 To finish the piece, press and lay flat to dry, finishing with a steam iron on wool setting when partly dry for a lovely smooth finish.

32 Sew a complementary backing fabric to your flat felt cushion cover and insert a cushion to complete the project.

scarf

scarf

MATERIALS Merino wool tops (shown here from Treetops Color Harmonies in a shade called Spring Swing). Decorative knitting yarn for surface decoration.

QUANTITY 2 oz of wool tops in total.

LAID-OUT SIZE 49" x 12". FINISHED SIZE 37" x 9".

Laying out

2

1 Work on the smooth side of the felting mat.

2 Gently pull a manageable length off the wool tops, then tease the wool apart in small tufts.

3 Lay these tufts side by side and row by row, slightly overlapping them as you go (the way roof tiles are laid).

4 Continue to lay out in this manner to reach the desired size of the first layer (49" x 12").

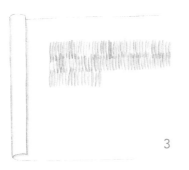

3

5 Lay out a second layer at right angles to the first. Fully cover the first layer. Two layers are sufficient for a scarf or it becomes too wide and bulky.

6 Decorate by laying knitting yarn in a spiral design on the surface of the laid-out wool tops.

7 Cover the laid-out fleece with netting.

Wetting down the fleece

8 Fill a plastic bottle that has holes in the lid with warm water and a few drops of detergent. Carefully shake this mixture over your work to wet down the fleece.

9 With your hand inside a plastic bag, rub the wetted area very gently in a circular motion.

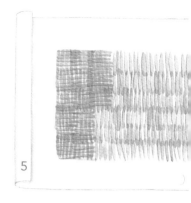

5

decorative yarn

6

Work from the middle towards the edges to avoid moving the pieces around. *Work very slowly and gently* – you do not want to disturb what you've just laid out. Continue until the entire piece is flat and wet but not dripping – *dry areas will not felt*.

10 Very gently remove the net, lifting carefully at the corners and gently pulling away the wool that catches (it will catch because it starts to felt to the net if you rub too vigorously).

11 To keep areas of detail undisturbed while rolling, lay a fine plastic drop sheet over your work, and gently press the plastic into place.

12 Roll the piece up in the felting mat and place rubber bands around the ends of the roll to keep it secure.

Rolling the felt

13 Lay a folded towel on the table and place the rolled felting mat on top of it – this is to soak up the drips and to stop the felting mat from slipping as you roll.

14 Roll the felting mat forward and backward 50 times, then unroll and check that the work hasn't moved (it's unlikely to have done so if covered with a sheet of plastic).

15 Gently reposition any pieces that have moved, then re-roll the felting mat from the opposite direction. Repeat the rolling and checking process three more times, rolling 50 times each time and re-rolling from the opposite end each time.

16 Repeat the rolling and checking process twice more, but roll 200 times each time.

17 Unroll and gently fold the wool into a small parcel and squeeze out the water.

18 Reheat the felt by dipping it in hot water and squeezing out the excess.

19 Unfold the felt, reposition it on the felting mat, and roll up quickly to retain the heat.

20 Roll another 200 times, unroll and check. Repeat twice, re-rolling from the opposite end of the felting mat each time. You will see the wool starting to shrink up and go bubbly and lumpy like pebbles – this is good, it's what we want. The scarf will have shrunk mostly in length because it has not been rolled from side to side.

Fulling the felt

By now the felt should be strong enough to be 'thrown'. If you're not sure then roll another 200 times.

21 Fold the wet felt into a small parcel and squeeze out all the water.

22 Throw this parcel with all your might against a towel on your work table or on the floor. Refold it when it comes undone and repeat this throwing process about 20 times – you will see the felt begin to shrink rapidly.

23 Turn the felting mat to bubble side up. Unfold the wet felt and reposition it on the mat surface. If the felt is dry, sprinkle with warm soapy water.

24 Place your hands on the surface of the felt and gently manipulate it with a light pressure, moving the felt against the rough bubbles, using the surface like

an old-fashioned washboard. This kneading process 'fulls' the felt causing rapid shrinkage as the bubbles act like a massager, gently moving the wool fibers against each other.

25 Continue to heat and manipulate the felt either by rolling or kneading until you have achieved the desired shrinkage and density.

26 To strengthen the edges of the felt roll them under your hand against the bubbles of the felting mat.

27 Rinse the felt with a solution of vinegar and water (half a cup of vinegar to a bucket of water) to remove the soap.

28 To finish the piece, press and lay flat to dry, finishing with a steam iron on wool setting when partly dry for a lovely smooth finish.

table runner

table runner by Kitty Chung O'Kane

MATERIALS Green and orange Merino wool tops.
QUANTITY 2¾ oz of wool tops in total.
LAID-OUT SIZE 47" x 23½". FINISHED SIZE 37" x 13½".

Laying out

1 Work on the smooth side of the felting mat.

2 Gently pull a manageable length off the
   green wool tops, then tease the wool apart
   in small tufts.

3 Lay these tufts side by side and row by row,
   slightly overlapping them as you go (the way
   roof tiles are laid).

4 Lay out to 47" x 23½", creating three
   fine layers, each layer at right angles to the
   one beneath it.

5 Very carefully cut random straight lines through
   the layers of wool with scissors – as if you are
   cutting up a jigsaw puzzle.

6 Very carefully push the cut pieces apart so there is ½–1" of space between all of the pieces but the overall shape is still rectangular.

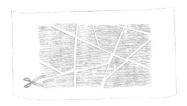

6

7 Use a contrasting or complementary color (the runner pictured uses orange) and lay a further two layers on top of the jigsaw pieces, placing each layer at right angles to the previous one, so that you are covering the green wool pieces as well as the spaces created by the cuts.

8 Cover the laid-out fleece with netting.

Wetting down the fleece

9 Fill a plastic bottle that has holes in the lid with warm water and a few drops of detergent. Carefully shake this mixture over your work to wet down the fleece.

10 With your hand inside a plastic bag, rub the wetted area very gently in a circular motion. Work from the middle towards the edges to avoid moving the pieces around. Continue until the entire piece is flat and wet but not dripping – dry areas will not felt.

11 Very gently remove the net,
    lifting carefully at the corners
    and pulling away the wool that
    catches (it will catch because
    it starts to felt to the net if you
    rub too vigorously).

12 To keep areas of detail
    undisturbed while rolling,
    lay a fine plastic drop sheet
    over your work, and gently
    press the plastic into place.

13 Roll the piece up in the felting
    mat and place rubber bands
    around the ends of the roll
    to keep it secure.

Rolling the felt

14 Lay a folded towel on the table
    and place the rolled felting mat
    on top of it – this is to soak up
    the drips and to stop the felting
    mat from slipping as you roll.

15 Roll the felting mat forward
    and backward 50 times, then
    unroll and check that the work
    hasn't moved (it's unlikely to
    have done so if covered with
    a sheet of plastic).

16 Gently reposition any pieces
    that have moved, then repeat
    the rolling and checking process
    three more times, re-rolling from
    the opposite end of the felting
    mat and rolling 50 times each time.

17 Repeat the rolling and checking
    process twice more, but roll
    200 times each time. Check and
    reposition any pieces that have
    moved before re-rolling.

18 Cut a paper pattern in the shape of your table runner – this one is a rectangle 47" x 23½".

19 Unroll the felting mat, pin the paper pattern to the wet wool and cut the felt to this size. Cut small triangle shapes out of the orange area (this repeats the triangle design) and remove them.

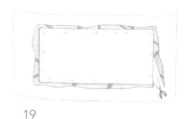

19

20 Now gently fold the wool into a small parcel and squeeze out the water.

21 Reheat the felt by dipping it in hot water and squeezing out the excess.

22 Unfold the felt, reposition it on the felting mat, and roll up quickly to retain the heat.

23 Roll another 200 times, unroll and check twice more, re-rolling from the opposite end of the felting mat each time. You will see the wool starting to shrink up and go bubbly and lumpy like pebbles – this is good, it's what we want.

Fulling the felt

By now the felt should be strong enough to be 'thrown'. If you're not sure then roll another 200 times.

24 Fold the wet felt into a small parcel and squeeze out the water.

25 Throw this parcel against a towel on your work table or on the floor. Refold when it comes undone. Repeat this throwing process about 20 times – you will see the felt begin to shrink rapidly.

26 Turn the felting mat to bubble side up. Unfold the wet felt and reposition it on the mat surface. If the felt is dry, sprinkle with warm soapy water.

27 Place your hands on the surface of the felt and gently manipulate it with a light pressure, moving the felt against the rough bubbles, using the surface like an old-fashioned washboard. This kneading process 'fulls' the felt causing rapid shrinkage as the bubbles act like a massager, gently moving the wool fibers against each other.

28 Continue to heat and manipulate the felt either by rolling or kneading until you have achieved the desired shrinkage and density.

29 To strengthen the edges of the felt roll them under your hand against the bubbles of the felting mat.

30 Rinse the felt with a solution of vinegar and water (half a cup of vinegar to a bucket of water) to remove the soap.

31 To finish, press and lay flat to dry, finishing with a steam iron on wool setting when partly dry.

picture

Start with a small sketch of the picture you want to create. Think about the areas of color and the different colored wool tops you will use for each area. You should use the fibers like brush strokes and decide which direction you want these to run. Have the picture framed with or without glass, or mount it as a wall hanging.

picture

MATERIALS A range of rainbow-dyed Merino wool tops in greens and blues, embroidered with very fine embroidery wool.
QUANTITY 1¾ oz of wool tops in total.
LAID-OUT SIZE 29″ x 19½″. FINISHED SIZE 22″ x 14½″.

2

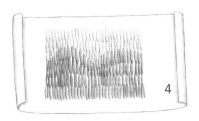

4

Laying out

1 Work on the smooth side of the felting mat.

2 Gently pull a manageable length off the wool tops, then tease the wool apart in small tufts.

3 Lay these tufts side by side and row by row, slightly overlapping them as you go (the way roof tiles are laid).

4 Continue to lay out in this manner using two areas of color – about a third in blue for sky and about two thirds in green for

the hills – with the fibers running up and down the picture.

5   Lay the second layer with the fibers running across the picture, following the colors from the first layer.

6   Lay a third green layer that follows the curve of the hills – the hills have one more layer than the sky.

7   Create treetops by winding spirals out of wool tops, and then add small brown lengths to create tree trunks – lay these in place on the picture.

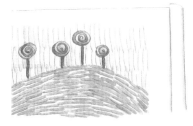

7

8   Cover the laid-out fleece with netting.

Wetting down the fleece

9   Fill a plastic bottle that has holes in the lid with warm water and a few drops of detergent. Carefully shake this mixture over your work to wet down the fleece.

10 With your hand inside a plastic bag, rub the wetted area very gently in a circular motion.

Work from the middle towards the edges to avoid moving the pieces around. *Work very slowly and gently* – you do not want to disturb what you've just laid out. Continue until the entire piece is flat and wet but not dripping *– dry areas will not felt.*

11 Very gently remove the net, lifting carefully at the corners and gently pulling away the wool that catches (it will catch because it starts to felt to the net if you rub too vigorously).

12 To keep areas of detail undisturbed while rolling, lay a fine plastic drop sheet over your work, and gently press the plastic into place.

13 Roll the piece up in the felting mat and place rubber bands around the ends of the roll to keep it secure.

Rolling the felt

14 Lay a folded towel on the table and place the rolled felting mat on top of it – this is to soak up the drips and to stop the felting mat from slipping as you roll.

15 Roll the felting mat forward and backward 50 times, then unroll and check that the work hasn't moved (it's unlikely to have done so if covered with a sheet of plastic).

16 Gently reposition any pieces that have moved, then repeat the rolling and checking process three more times, turning the felt ninety degrees before re-rolling each time and rolling 50 times each time.

17 Repeat the rolling and checking process four more times. Reposition any pieces that have moved and turn the felt ninety degrees before re-rolling. Roll 200 times each time.

18 Unroll and gently fold the wool into a small parcel and squeeze out the water.

19 Reheat the felt by dipping it in hot water and squeezing out the excess.

20 Unfold the felt, reposition it on the felting mat, and roll up quickly to retain the heat.

21 Roll another 200 times, unroll and check. Repeat twice, re-rolling from the opposite end of the felting mat each time. You will see the wool starting to shrink up and go bubbly and lumpy like pebbles – this is good, it's what we want.

Fulling the felt

By now the felt should be strong enough to be 'thrown'. If you're not sure then roll another 200 times.

22 Fold the wet felt into a small parcel and squeeze out all the water.

23 Throw this parcel with all your might against a towel on your work table or on the floor. Refold it when it comes undone and repeat this throwing process about 20 times – you will see the felt begin to shrink rapidly.

24 Turn the felting mat to bubble side up. Unfold the wet felt and reposition it on the mat surface. If the felt is dry, sprinkle with warm soapy water.

25 Place your hands on the surface of the felt and gently manipulate it with a light pressure, moving the felt against the rough

bubbles, using the surface like an old-fashioned washboard. This kneading process 'fulls' the felt causing rapid shrinkage as the bubbles act like a massager, gently moving the wool fibers against each other.

26 Continue to heat and manipulate the felt either by rolling or kneading until you have achieved the desired shrinkage and density.

27 To strengthen the edges of the felt roll them under your hand against the bubbles of the felting mat.

28 Rinse the felt with a solution of vinegar and water (half a cup of vinegar to a bucket of water) to remove the soap.

29 To finish the piece, press and lay flat to dry, finishing with a steam iron when partly dry for a lovely smooth finish.

Embellishment

30 Use embroidery wool and running stitches to echo the shapes of the treetops and curves of the hill – this helps to add more dimension to your picture.

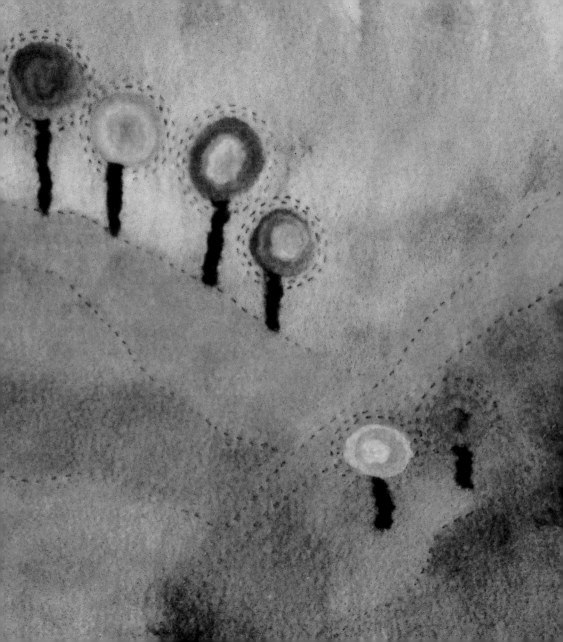

Once you've mastered the basics of making felt, you can start to explore its other amazing properties through more advanced techniques, such as using pre-felt.

Pre-felt is partially rolled felt that has only just begun to matt together. Working with pre-felted pieces opens up more choices of pattern and design. Sharp lines, precise patterns and strong definition between colors are created through the pre-felt technique of cutting, layering and joining different colored and shaped pieces. A mixture of plain and textured pre-felt pieces gives the finished work a rich and interesting surface.

Make dozens of different pre-felted pieces to prepare for a project, allow them to dry, so you can sit, stitch and join them later. You can work with them wet if necessary, although it is easier when they are dry and there is less chance of them tearing.

pre-felts

When stitching pre-felt pieces together use a chenille needle. It has a big eye to hold knitting yarn or embroidery wool but has a sharp point. I work with wool because it will felt into the surface – you can see the stitches, but you can't feel them. Cotton or silk thread will ripple across the surface as the wool shrinks – an interesting effect. Pre-felt pieces do not have to be stitched together if overlapped when laid out, but I often put in a few 'security' stitches with cotton or nylon sewing thread (which I pull out later) to ensure that the pieces don't move.

The projects that follow use pre-felts in a variety of ways, some laid out with wool tops and rolled as described for flat felt, others using carded wool batts. Wool batts are more expensive than wool tops, but the laying out is done for you.

The baby blanket project includes instructions on how to prepare pre-felts; these principles apply to all of the pre-felt projects that follow.

baby blanket

This is a modern variation on the tradition of creating embroidered woolen blankets as gifts for newborn babies. The finished blanket can be embroidered with the baby's name after felting. Three pieces of pre-felt are stitched together to form the blanket, and then small pre-felt squares are stitched on top.

baby blanket

MATERIALS As shown, merino wool batts from Margaret Peel's Fiber Supplies and silk hankies from Treetops Color Harmonies. Fine knitting yarn for embroidery.

QUANTITY 5 oz of wool in total.

LAID-OUT SIZE 39" x 21½". FINISHED SIZE 31" x 17½". The total laid-out size comprises a white rectangle 19½" x 21½" in the center, and two purple rectangles measuring 10" x 21½" at each end. You will also need to create a selection of pre-felts from which to cut decorative squares. This project has used four different colored pre-felts (blue, green, red and purple) from which squares about 3" x 3" are cut.

Laying out pre-felts using wool tops

1 Work on the smooth side of the felting mat.

2 Gently pull a manageable length off the wool tops, then tease the wool apart in small tufts.

2

3 Lay these tufts side by side and row by row, slightly overlapping them as you go (the way roof tiles are laid).

4　Continue to lay out in this manner until you have reached the desired size of each main piece (center piece 19½" x 21½" in white; two end pieces 10" x 21½" in purple).

5　Place a second layer at right angles to and fully covering the first layer.

6　Keep layering until you have reached the desired thickness (three or four layers are enough for this project).

7　Decorate the surface with silk, yarn, and other embellishments.

8　Cover the laid-out fleece with netting. *(See Wetting down the fleece to continue.)*

Laying out pre-felts – using wool batts

1　Gently unroll the wool batt – use as is or split in half for a finer piece of finished felt (I've used the batts at their full thickness for this project).

2　Decorate the surface with silk, yarn, and other embellishments.

3　Cover the laid-out batt with netting.

Wetting down the fleece

9　Fill a plastic bottle with holes in the lid with warm water and a few drops of detergent. Shake this mixture over your work to wet down the fleece.

10　With your hand inside a plastic bag, rub the wetted area very gently in a circular motion. Work from the middle towards the edges to avoid moving the pieces around. *Work very slowly and gently.* Continue until the entire piece is flat and wet but not dripping – *dry areas will not felt.*

11 Very gently remove the net, lifting carefully at the corners and gently pulling away the wool that catches (it will catch because it starts to felt to the net if you rub too vigorously).

12 Roll the piece up in the felting mat and place rubber bands around the ends of the roll to keep it secure.

Rolling the pre-felt

Pre-felts are only partially felted at this stage. Felting is completed after the pieces have been joined.

13 Place the rolled up felting mat on a towel and roll forward and backward 50 times. Unroll the mat and check that the work hasn't moved – gently reposition pieces if necessary. Repeat the rolling and checking process four more times, turning the felt ninety degrees before re-rolling each time and rolling 50 times each time.

14 Unroll and gently fold the wool into a small parcel and squeeze out all of the water. Then lay the piece out flat to dry without rinsing, unless it will be stored for a very long time, in which case rinse first.

Piecing the pre-felts

15 When the pre-felt pieces are dry, carefully cut the pieces for your project with sharp fabric scissors – remembering that the whole piece still has to shrink when it is felted later.

16 Working on the smooth side of the felting mat, take the three main pieces for the blanket and butt them together using a 'whip' stitch and cotton or nylon sewing thread. This thread will be pulled out after the piece is felted and has dried. Pull the stitches firmly, with no slack – when the wool is wet down again it will spread apart, if the pieces of pre-felt are not pulled closely together you will have holes in your work.

17 Place the decorative squares on the surface and anchor each square in place with a running stitch. Use another row of running stitch to outline each square.

18 Cover the felt with netting.

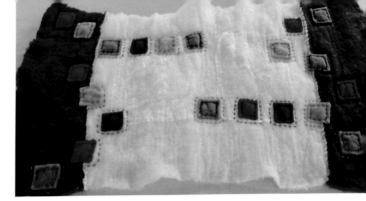

Re-wetting the pre-felts

19 Repeat the wetting down process as described above. It will take more water this time because you have more layers of wool to wet.

20 Place a mesh bag over sections of the felt and use the wooden trowel to rub the pieces into place.

21 To keep areas of detail undisturbed while rolling, lay a fine plastic drop sheet over your work, and gently press the plastic into place.

22 Roll the piece up in the felting mat, and place rubber bands around the ends of the roll to keep it secure.

Rolling the felt

23 Lay a folded towel on the table and place the rolled felting mat on top of it.

24 Roll the felting mat forward and backward 50 times, then unroll and check that the work hasn't moved (it's unlikely to have done so if covered with a sheet of plastic).

25 Gently reposition any pieces that have moved, then re-roll the felting mat from the opposite direction. Repeat the rolling and checking process three more times, rolling 50 times each time and re-rolling from the opposite direction each time.

26 Repeat the rolling and checking process twice more, re-rolling from opposite ends each time and rolling 200 times each time.

27 Unroll and gently fold the wool into a small parcel and squeeze out the water.

28 Reheat the felt by dipping it in hot water and squeezing out the excess.

29 Unfold the felt, reposition it on the felting mat, and roll up quickly to retain the heat.

30 Roll 200 times, unroll and check. Repeat twice, re-rolling from the opposite end of the felting mat each time and rolling 200 times each time. You will see the wool starting to shrink up and go bubbly and lumpy like pebbles – this is good, it's what we want.

Fulling the felt

By now the felt should be strong enough to be 'thrown'. If you're not sure then roll another 200 times.

31 Fold the wet felt into a small parcel and squeeze out all the water.

32 Throw this parcel with all your might against a towel on your work table or on the floor. Refold it when it comes undone and repeat this throwing process about 20 times – you will see the felt begin to shrink rapidly.

33 Turn the felting mat to bubble side up. Unfold the wet felt and reposition it on the mat surface. If the felt is dry, sprinkle with warm soapy water.

34 Place your hands on the surface of the felt and gently manipulate it with a light pressure, moving the felt against the rough bubbles, using the surface like an old-fashioned washboard. This kneading process 'fulls' the felt causing rapid shrinkage as the bubbles act like a massager, gently moving the wool fibers against each other.

35 Continue to heat and manipulate the felt either by rolling or kneading until you have achieved the desired shrinkage and density.

36 To strengthen the edges of the felt roll them under your hand against the bubbles of the felting mat.

37 Rinse the felt with a solution of vinegar and water (half a cup of vinegar to a bucket of water) to remove the soap.

38 To finish the piece, press and lay flat to dry, finishing with a steam iron on wool setting when partly dry for a smooth finish.

scarf with flowers

This stunning scarf uses the flat felt technique to create a background onto which pre-felt flowers are placed. Make your scarf as long or as short as you like. Change the motif from flowers to spirals or hearts, whatever you like.

scarf with flowers

MATERIALS The scarf pictured was made with Merino wool tops from Yarn Barn, using pre-felt flowers in pink, orange, yellow and with black centers.
QUANTITY 2½ oz of wool for the scarf background; 1 oz of each color for the pre-felt flowers, laid out in two layers.
LAID-OUT SIZE 117" x 12". FINISHED SIZE 68" x 9".

Laying out

Prepare pre-felts for the flowers, laying out several small pieces at once to save time. Refer to the baby blanket project for instructions on how to create pre-felt pieces (p. 51).

2

1 Work on the smooth side of the felting mat.

2 Lay out the area for the background of the scarf to the desired size, 117" x 12" – I've used purple wool tops. Make sure the scarf is fairly narrow so it's not too bulky around your neck.
Pull tufts from the wool tops and lay out side by side and row by row, overlapping them as you go.

3 Lay out a second layer at right angles to the first. Two layers are sufficient for a scarf or it becomes too wide and bulky.

4 Cut the pre-felt flower shapes and black flower centers using the templates provided (*see page 120*) and place them on the purple fleece. Position them carefully along the length of the scarf because it's very difficult to move them from the soft unfelted wool underneath. Place the black centers in the middle of the flower shapes.

4

5 Cover the laid-out fleece with netting.

Wetting down the fleece

6 Fill a plastic bottle that has holes in the lid with warm water and a few drops of detergent. Carefully shake this mixture over your work to wet down the fleece.

7 With your hand inside a plastic bag, rub the wetted area very gently in a circular motion. Work from the middle towards the edges to avoid moving the pieces around. *Work very slowly and gently* – you do not want to

disturb what you've just laid out. Continue until the entire piece is flat and wet but not dripping – *dry areas will not felt*.

8 Very gently remove the net, lifting carefully at the corners and gently pulling away the wool that catches (it will catch because it starts to felt to the net if you rub too vigorously).

9 To keep areas of detail undisturbed while rolling, lay a fine plastic drop sheet over your work and gently press the plastic into place.

10 Roll the piece up in the felting mat and place rubber bands around the ends of the roll to keep it secure.

Rolling the felt

11 Lay a folded towel on the table and place the rolled felting mat on top of it – this is to soak up the drips and to stop the felting mat from slipping as you roll.

12 Roll the felting mat forward and backward 50 times, then unroll and check that the work hasn't moved (it's unlikely to have done so if covered with a layer of plastic).

13 Gently reposition any pieces that have moved, then re-roll the felting mat from the opposite direction and repeat the rolling and checking process three more times, rolling 50 times each time and re-rolling from the opposite end of the felting mat each time.

14 Re-roll the felting mat and roll 200 times, then unroll and check again, replacing any pieces that have moved. Re-roll the felting

mat from the opposite direction and repeat the rolling and checking process twice more, rolling 200 times each time and re-rolling from the opposite end of the felting mat each time.

15 Unroll and gently fold the wool into a small parcel and squeeze out the water.

16 Reheat the wool by dipping your work in hot water and squeezing out the excess.

17 Unfold the felt, reposition it on the felting mat and roll up quickly to retain the heat.

18 Roll another 200 times, unroll and check. Repeat twice, re-rolling from the opposite end of the felting mat each time. You will see the wool starting to shrink up and go bubbly and lumpy like pebbles – this is good, it's what we want. The scarf will have shrunk mostly

in length because it has not been rolled from side to side.

Fulling the felt

By now the felt should be strong enough to be 'thrown'. If you're not sure then roll another 200 times.

19 Fold the wet felt into a small parcel and squeeze out all the water.

20 Throw this parcel with all your might against a towel on your work table or on the floor. Refold it when it comes undone and repeat this throwing process about 20 times – you will see the felt begin to shrink rapidly.

21 Turn the felting mat to bubble side up. Unfold the wet felt and reposition it on the mat surface. If the felt is dry, sprinkle with warm soapy water.

22 Place your hands on the surface of the felt and gently manipulate it with a light pressure, moving the felt against the rough bubbles, using the surface like an old-fashioned washboard. This kneading process 'fulls' the felt causing rapid shrinkage as the bubbles act like a massager, gently moving the wool fibers against each other.

23 Continue to heat and manipulate the felt either by rolling or kneading until you have achieved the desired shrinkage and density.

24 To strengthen the edges of the felt roll them under your hand against the bubbles of the felting mat.

25 Rinse the felt with a solution of vinegar and water (half a cup of vinegar to a bucket of water) to remove the soap.

26 To finish the piece, press and lay flat to dry, finishing with a steam iron on wool setting when partly dry for a lovely smooth finish.

cushion with
squares

Look at interiors magazines for the latest color and design trends and inspiration for creating your own funky cushions. They don't take too long to make, so you can change them with the seasons. The trick is to keep the designs simple so that the finished product is uncluttered but striking.

cushion with squares

MATERIALS A variety of Merino wool tops and Merino batts. The important thing is the colors: I made up a variety of pre-felt pieces in lime, turquoise, green and blue.

QUANTITY 1¾ oz each of lime and blue wool, and 1 oz each of turquoise and green, laid out in two layers to make pre-felts.

LAID-OUT SIZE 25" x 25". FINISHED SIZE 19" x 19".

Laying out

Prepare the pre-felts for the cushion in a variety of colors. I used silk tops and old silk scarves to create subtle textured areas on some pieces. Lay out several pieces at once to save time. Refer to the baby blanket project for instructions on how to create pre-felt pieces (p. 51).

1 Create four pre-felt pieces from which to make the cushion: lime (25" x 25"), blue (25" x 25"), turquoise (12½" x 25") and green (12½" x 12½").

2 Let the pre-felt pieces dry and then lay them all out on your table to select the areas you want to use.

3 Cut two 12½" x 25" rectangles from the pre-felt; I used lime and blue pre-felt. Place them side by side along the long edge and butt them together using a 'whip' stitch with nylon or cotton sewing thread. This thread will be pulled out after the piece is felted and dry. Pull the stitches firmly, with no slack – when the wool is wet down it will spread apart, so the stitches need to hold it together.

4 Cut four squares approximately 7" x 7" and place these on the joined rectangles. The cushion pictured used two turquoise squares and one each of lime and green.

5 Cut sixteen thin strips about 6" x ¾" and position these on the squares. I've used blue pre-felt. These can be stitched in place if you choose, with either decorative wool, or a thread that can be pulled out later.

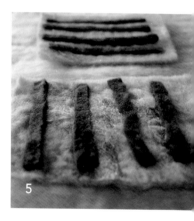

6 Cover the finished design with netting.

Wetting down the fleece

7 Fill a plastic bottle that has holes in the lid with warm water and a few drops of detergent.

Carefully shake this mixture over your work to wet down the fleece.

8 With your hand inside a plastic bag, rub the wetted area very gently in a circular motion. Work from the middle towards the edges to avoid moving the pieces around. *Work very slowly and gently* – you do not want to disturb what you've just laid out. Continue until the entire piece is flat and wet but not dripping *– dry areas will not felt.*

9 Very gently remove the net, lifting carefully at the corners and gently pulling away the wool that catches (it will catch because it starts to felt to the net if you rub too vigorously).

10 To keep areas of detail undisturbed while rolling lay a fine plastic drop sheet over your work and gently press the plastic into place.

11 Roll the piece up in the felting mat and place rubber bands around the ends of the roll to keep it secure.

Rolling the felt

12 Lay a folded towel on the table and place the rolled felting mat on top of it – this is to soak up the drips and to stop the felting mat from slipping as you roll.

13 Roll the felting mat forward and backward 50 times, then unroll and check that the work hasn't moved (it's unlikely to have done so if covered with a layer of plastic).

14 Gently reposition any pieces that have moved, then repeat the rolling and checking process three more times, turning the felt ninety degrees between turns and rolling 50 times each time.

15 Repeat the rolling and checking process four more times, turning the felt ninety degrees each time and rolling 200 times each time. Reposition any pieces that have moved each time you check your work.

16 Unroll and gently fold the wool into a small parcel and squeeze out the water.

17 Reheat the wool by dipping your work in hot water and squeezing out the excess.

18 Unfold the felt, reposition it on the felting mat and roll up quickly to retain the heat.

19 Roll another 200 times, unroll and check. Repeat twice, turning the felt ninety degrees each time and rolling 200 times each time. You will see the wool starting to shrink up and go bubbly and lumpy like pebbles – this is what we want.

Fulling the felt

By now the felt should be strong enough to be 'thrown'. If you're not sure then roll another 200 times.

20 Fold the wet felt into a small parcel and squeeze out the water.

21 Throw this parcel with all your might against a towel on your work table or on the floor. Refold it when it comes undone and repeat this throwing process about 20 times – you will see the felt begin to shrink rapidly.

22 Turn the felting mat to bubble side up. Unfold the wet felt and reposition it on the mat surface. If the felt is dry, sprinkle with warm soapy water.

23 Place your hands on the surface of the felt and gently manipulate it with a light pressure, moving the felt against the rough bubbles, using the surface like

an old-fashioned washboard. This kneading process 'fulls' the felt causing rapid shrinkage as the bubbles act like a massager, gently moving the wool fibers against each other.

24 Continue to heat and manipulate the felt either by rolling or kneading until you have achieved the desired shrinkage and density.

25 To strengthen the edges of the felt roll them under your hand against the bubbles of the felting mat.

26 Rinse the felt with a solution of vinegar and water (half a cup of vinegar to a bucket of water) to remove the soap.

27 To finish the piece, press and lay flat to dry, finishing with a steam iron on wool setting when partly dry for a lovely smooth finish.

28 Sew a complementary backing fabric to your felt design and insert a cushion to complete the project.

decorative flags

This project is a wonderful way to show off your felting and design skills, and to explore new ideas. To create different surfaces and patterns try embroidery before and after felting and use a variety of silks and other fabrics to add texture. In this project, more is more.

decorative flags

MATERIALS A variety of Merino wool tops and Merino batts. Texture has been added to the surface with silk tops, silk hankies, silk scarves, wool nops, knitting yarn and spiral-dyed wool tops. The important thing is to experiment – and create a range of patterned and plain pre-felt pieces.

QUANTITY 5¼ oz of wool in pinks, yellows and reds.

LAID-OUT SIZE Template for flag measures 8" x 11¾"; lay out a total area of at least 29" x 39" from which you can cut nine flags.

Laying out

Make up a variety of pre-felt pieces in a variety of textures and colors. Lay out several pieces at once to save time. Two layers are best so the flags stay soft and drapable. Refer to the baby blanket project for instructions on how to create pre-felt pieces (p. 51).

1 Create a total area of pre-felt in various colors (I've used light pink, dark pink, yellow and red) of at least 29" x 39" from which to cut your flag shapes.

2 Cut nine flag shapes, using the template provided as a guideline (*p. 121*), or make up your own flag shape. The template allows for shrinkage.

3 Decorate the surface of each pre-felt flag with silk, yarn, and other embellishments. Cut out letters from the pre-felt scraps and stitch into place on the flag shapes. Add decorative stitches – remember that more is more.

4 Place all the flag shapes on your felting mat and cover with netting.

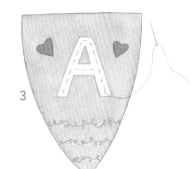

3

Wetting down the fleece

5 Fill a plastic bottle that has holes in the lid with warm water and a few drops of detergent. Carefully shake this mixture over your work to wet down the fleece.

6 With your hand inside a plastic bag, rub the wetted area very gently in a circular motion. Work from the middle towards the edges to avoid moving the pieces around. *Work very slowly and gently* – you do not want to disturb

what you've just laid out. Continue until the entire piece is flat and wet but not dripping – *dry areas will not felt*.

7 Very gently remove the net, lifting carefully at the corners and gently pulling away the wool that catches (it will catch because it starts to felt to the net if you rub too vigorously).

8 To keep areas of detail undisturbed while rolling, lay a fine plastic drop sheet over your work and gently press the plastic into place.

9 Roll the piece up in the felting mat and place rubber bands around the ends of the roll to keep it secure.

Rolling the felt

10 Lay a folded towel on the table and place the rolled felting mat on top of it – to soak up the drips and to stop the felting mat from slipping as you roll.

11 Roll the felting mat forward and backward 50 times, then unroll and check that the work hasn't moved (it's unlikely to have done so if covered with a layer of plastic).

12 Gently reposition any pieces that have moved, then re-roll the felting mat from the opposite direction and repeat the rolling and checking process three more times, re-rolling from the opposite end of the felting mat each time and rolling 50 times each time.

13 Re-roll the felting mat from the opposite direction and repeat the rolling and checking process

twice more, re-rolling from the opposite end of the felting mat and rolling 200 times each time.

14 Unroll and gently fold the wool into a small parcel and squeeze out the water.

15 Reheat the wool by dipping your work in hot water and squeezing out the excess.

16 Unfold the felt, reposition it on the felting mat and roll up quickly to retain the heat.

17 Roll another 200 times, unroll and check. Repeat twice, re-rolling from the opposite end of the felting mat each time. You will see the wool starting to shrink up and go bubbly and lumpy like pebbles – this is good, it's what we want.

Fulling the felt

By now the felt should be strong enough to be 'thrown'. If you're not sure then roll another 200 times. The flags should be fulled separately or in groups of two or three at a time. The last part of the fulling needs to be worked individually for each flag. Make sure you pull them back into shape before they dry so that the shape of the flags is uniform.

18 Fold the wet felt into a small parcel and squeeze out all the water.

19 Throw this parcel with all your might against a towel on your work table or on the floor. Refold it when it comes undone and repeat this throwing process about 20 times – you will see the felt begin to shrink rapidly.

20 Turn the felting mat to bubble side up. Unfold the wet felt and reposition it on the mat surface.

If the felt is dry, sprinkle with warm soapy water.

21 Place your hands on the surface of the felt and gently manipulate it with a light pressure, moving the felt against the rough bubbles, using the surface like an old-fashioned washboard. This kneading process 'fulls' the felt causing rapid shrinkage as the bubbles act like a massager, gently moving the wool fibers against each other.

22 Continue to heat and manipulate the felt either by rolling or kneading until you have achieved the desired shrinkage and density.

23 To strengthen the edges of the felt roll them under your hand against the bubbles of the felting mat.

24 Rinse the felt with a solution of vinegar and water (half a cup of vinegar to a bucket or water) to remove the soap.

25 To finish the piece, press and lay flat to dry, finishing with a steam iron on wool setting when partly dry for a lovely smooth finish.

To make up the flags

26 To make a felt cord follow the steps below.

27 Lay a towel on the table, then place a matchstick blind on top. If you only have a pool cover, work on the bubble side.

28 Pull off a 70" length of wool tops and wet down either by dipping into sludge, or using the shaker bottle.

29 Place the length of wool tops parallel to the ridges on the blind and roll this like a long sausage with your hands.

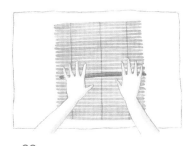

29

30 When the wool tops start to form a cord shape, pick up the edge of the blind, fold it over the cord and start rolling the blind with the cord positioned under the palm of your hand inside the fold of the blind.

31 Roll firmly until the cord is hard and smooth.

32 Unroll the blind and continue to full the cord by heating, throwing and massaging by hand.

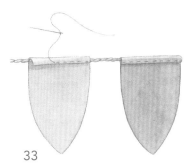

33 Lay the flags face down in the order that they should hang. Place the cord along the top of the flags, fold over the top of each flag and stitch in place to enclose the cord.

33

bag

This is the easiest bag design in the world: a flat felt square with pre-felt pieces laid on top. The bag is created by folding two opposite corners together and hand stitching the seam. The flap is rolled up to create detail, with a snap fastener stitched underneath to close it, and a felt cord is attached to make a strap.

bag by Elizabeth Armstrong

MATERIALS Merino wool tops. The bag shown is made from tops Elizabeth dyed herself. Leaf-shaped pre-felt pieces are applied to the laid-out fleece to give interesting detail. Further texture could be added by using machine embroidery to emphasise the leaf shapes.

QUANTITY 2¾ oz of wool in total for the pre-felt leaves, bag and handle.

LAID-OUT SIZE 19½" x 19½" for the bag, plus a 51" length for the cord.

FINISHED SIZE 13" x 13" bag, 47" cord.

Laying out

Prepare green pre-felt pieces from which to cut leaf shapes. Refer to the baby blanket project on how to create the pre-felt pieces (p. 51).

1 Work on the smooth side of the felting mat.

2 To make the main body of the bag gently pull a manageable length off the wool tops, then tease the wool apart in small tufts.

2

3 Lay these tufts side by side and row by row, slightly overlapping them as you go (the way roof tiles are laid).

4 Continue to lay out in this manner until you have reached the desired size of the first layer (19½" x 19½").

5 Lay out a second layer so it fully covers the first, but is laid out at right angles to the bottom layer.

6 Repeat this with more layers, depending on the thickness desired from the finished felt (three or four layers for this project).

7 Decorate the fleece by laying silk, yarn, and other details on the surface to embellish your design as required.

8 Cut pre-felt leaf shapes and lay them out at random across the piece. Don't move them once placed or you'll disturb the soft unfelted wool underneath.

9 When finished, cover the design with netting.

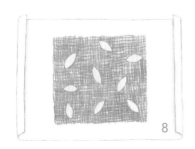

8

Wetting down the fleece

10 Fill a plastic bottle that has holes in the lid with warm water and a few drops of detergent. Carefully shake this mixture over your work to wet down the fleece.

11 With your hand inside a plastic bag, rub the wetted area very gently in a circular motion. Work from the middle towards the edges to avoid moving the pieces around. *Work very slowly and gently* – you do not want to disturb what you've just laid out. Continue until the entire piece is flat and wet but not dripping – *dry areas will not felt.*

12 Very gently remove the net, lifting carefully at the corners and gently pulling away the wool that catches (it will catch because it starts to felt to the net if you rub too vigorously).

13 To keep areas of detail undisturbed while rolling, lay a fine plastic drop sheet over your work and gently press the plastic into place.

14 Roll the piece up in the felting mat and place rubber bands around the ends of the roll to keep it secure.

Rolling the felt

15 Lay a folded towel on the table and place the rolled felting mat on top of it – this is to soak up the drips and to stop the felting mat from slipping as you roll.

16 Roll the felting mat forward and backward 50 times, then unroll and check that the work hasn't moved (it's unlikely to have done so if covered with a layer of plastic).

17 Gently reposition any pieces that have moved, then repeat the rolling and checking process three more times, turning the felt ninety degrees between turns, and rolling 50 times each time.

18 Repeat the rolling and checking process four more times, turning the felt ninety degrees between turns and rolling 200 times each time. Reposition any pieces that have moved each time you check your work.

19 Unroll and gently fold the wool into a small parcel and squeeze out the water.

20 Reheat the wool by dipping your work in hot water and squeezing out the excess.

21 Unfold the felt, reposition it on the felting mat and roll up quickly to retain the heat.

22 Roll another 200 times, unroll and check. Repeat twice, re-rolling from the opposite end of the felting mat each time. You will see the wool starting to shrink up and go bubbly and lumpy like pebbles – this is good, it's what we want.

Fulling the felt

By now the felt should be strong enough to be 'thrown'. If you're not sure then roll another 200 times.

23 Fold the wet felt into a small parcel and squeeze out all the water.

24 Throw this parcel with all your might against a towel on your work table or on the floor. Refold it when it comes undone and repeat this throwing process about 20 times – you will see the felt begin to shrink rapidly.

25 Turn the felting mat to bubble side up. Unfold the wet felt and reposition it on the mat surface. If the felt is dry, sprinkle with warm soapy water.

26 Place your hands on the surface of the felt and gently manipulate it with a light pressure, moving the felt against the rough bubbles, using the surface like an old-fashioned washboard. This kneading process 'fulls' the felt causing rapid shrinkage as the bubbles act like a massager, gently moving the wool fibers against each other.

27 Continue to heat and manipulate the felt either by rolling or kneading until you have achieved the desired shrinkage and density.

28 To strengthen the edges of the felt roll them under your hand against the bubbles of the felting mat.

29 Rinse the felt with a solution of vinegar and water (half a cup of vinegar to a bucket of water) to remove the soap.

wool tops

30 To finish the piece, press and lay flat to dry, finishing with a steam iron on wool setting when partly dry for a lovely smooth finish.

Embellishment

31 Add machine or hand embroidery before making up the bag if desired.

The cord

32 Lay a towel on the table, then place a matchstick blind on top. If you've only got a pool cover, work on the bubble side.

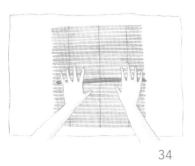

34

33 Pull off a 51" length of wool tops and wet down either by dipping into sludge, or using the shaker bottle.

34 Place the length of wool tops parallel to the ridges on the blind and with your hands roll this like a long sausage.

35 When it starts to form a cord shape, pick up the edge of the blind, fold it over the cord and start rolling with the cord under the palm of your hand inside the fold of the blind.

finished cord

36 Roll firmly inside the blind until it forms
a hard smooth cord.

37 Unroll the blind and continue to full the cord
by heating, throwing and massaging by hand.

To make up the bag

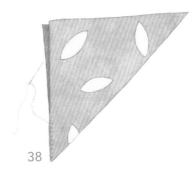

38 Fold two opposite corners together and hand
stitch this seam with a stitch that will bind the
bag together and give it strength. Elizabeth
has used blanket stitch with a fine thread.

38

39 Roll up the front edge of the top flap and
stitch into place with invisible stitches from
the under-side.

40 Stitch snap fastener or some other type
of sew-on closure under the flap, so you can
close your bag.

39

41 Stitch the felt cord to the outside or
inside of the bag for a handle or strap.

Nuno felt is a variation on flat felt with the addition of another material – fine open-weave fabric. Many different fabrics can be used, although natural fibers such as silk and cotton are the most successful. The combination of these materials with feltmaking techniques, where you manipulate the wool fiber through the weave of the fabric, creates a very strong but lightweight fabric. The characteristics are very different from normal felt, because this combination takes on a ruched and bubbled appearance, which is caused by the shrink of the wool and the non-shrink of the fabric.

Nuno felt is a technique devised by Polly Stirling. Polly lives in northern New South Wales and wanted to create lightweight felts that can be worn in tropical climates. Through experimentation Polly came up with this wonderful concept, which she called 'nuno', which means 'woven fabric' in Japanese. So nuno felt is literally felt on woven fabric.

nuno felt

Nuno felt possesses many wonderful qualities. It is strong but light, airy and drapable. It is versatile and can be used to create wraps, skirts, scarves, vests, jackets or floaty evening wear, or homewares such as window drapes, cushions, placemats, table runners and bed covers.

Fabrics that can be used to create nuno felt include silk gauze (tissue silk), silk organza or silk chiffon, cotton voile, scrim or gauze and old silk and cotton scarves.

Nuno felt also lends itself to a range of embellishment possibilities. Trap or collage other materials such as textured fabrics, leaves and lace between the wool and the fabric layers. Decorate the surface of the wool tops with silk fibers, fabric scraps, yarn or other threads chopped up into pieces (think fine and light). Stitch the finished item with hand or machine embroidery. With nuno felt you can experiment with anything that takes your fancy.

wrap

Gather up the prettiest, tackiest, biggest, oldest and tattiest silk scarves that you can find. These can be used to make wonderful new wraps, throws, scarves or skirts using the nuno felting technique.

This project has been made with a beautiful fine open-weave silk shawl from India as the base. The shawl measured 39" x 78" to start with, and with just one fine layer of wool tops it has become a gorgeous light and drapable wrap, measuring 23½" x 64½".

The silk fabric can be laid under or over the layer of wool, so lay out the fleece first then cover it with several small scarves if you can't get one big one. Use several fine layers of wool tops laid out at random if you prefer, or follow a structured design as I have with this piece.

wrap

MATERIALS Merino wool tops and a large, very open weave silk shawl purchased in an accessories shop.
QUANTITY 1¾ oz of wool in total.
LAID-OUT SIZE 39" x 78". FINISHED SIZE 23½" x 64½".

Laying out

1 Lay the scarf on the smooth side of your felting mat. Use masking tape to secure the corners of the fabric to the felting mat as it is being laid out.

2 Gently pull a manageable length off the wool tops, then tease the wool apart in small tufts and lay on top of the silk fabric in your chosen pattern. You do

not have to lay out in a structured pattern, as in basic flat felting, but can freely lay out the wool in any direction because of the structure and weave of the base fabric. I've used zig-zag patterns, waves and rings in three shades of blue. The more fleece you use to cover the fabric the more shrinkage you will get as the end result.

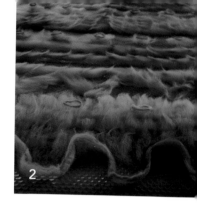

3 Continue to lay out in this manner until you have covered the silk scarf – I've left some areas with no fleece and other areas are covered entirely.

4 If you want a heavier coverage of wool, lay out a second light layer at right angles to the first layer or at random.

5 To create an interesting edge to the ends of the wrap, I have laid out fleece in a wave pattern so that some of the fleece is hanging off the edge onto the pool cover. This will stay in position if you look after it carefully during the wetting and rolling stages and cover it with a layer of light plastic.

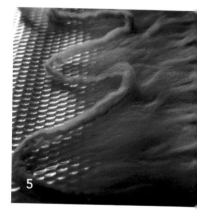

6 Decorate the surface by laying silk, yarn, and other embellishments on your design, if this is the effect that you want.

7 Remove the masking tape and cover the laid-out fleece with netting.

Wetting down the fleece

8 Fill a plastic bottle that has holes in the lid with cool water and detergent – with nuno felt you need a more soapy mixture to make the wool adhere to the base fabric. Carefully shake a small amount of this mixture onto the laid-out fleece.

9 With your hand inside a plastic bag, rub the lightly wetted fleece very gently in a circular motion. Work from the middle to the edges to avoid moving the pieces around. *Work very slowly and gently* – you do not want to disturb what you've just worked so hard to lay out. Continue until the entire piece is flat and moist, but not too wet – *dry areas will not felt.*

10 Very gently remove the net, lifting carefully at the corners and gently pulling away the wool that catches (it will catch because it starts to felt the net if you rub too vigorously).

11 Lay a sheet of fine plastic over your work and press it gently into place as if you are laminating the wool and silk between the plastic and the felting mat.

12 Roll the fleece up in the felting mat and place rubber bands around the ends of the roll to keep it secure.

Rolling the felt

Nuno felt takes more rolling than normal flat felt as there are fewer wool fibers to tangle and mat together.

13 Lay a folded towel on the table and place the rolled felting mat on top of it – this is to soak up the drips and to stop the felting mat from slipping as you roll.

14 Roll the felting mat forward and backward 100 times, then unroll and check that your work hasn't moved (it's unlikely to have done so if covered with a sheet of plastic).

15 Gently reposition any pieces that have moved, then re-roll the felting mat from the opposite direction. Repeat the rolling and checking process three more times, rolling 100 times each time and re-rolling from the opposite end each time.

16 Re-roll the felting mat and repeat the rolling and checking process four times, re-rolling from the opposite direction each time and rolling 200 times each time.

17 Unroll and carefully lift a corner of the plastic. Lift the silk very gently and check the back to see if the wool fibers have evenly penetrated the surface. If so, continue to the fulling stage. If not, continue rolling until the wool fibers evenly penetrate the fabric.

Fulling the felt

18 Gently fold the wet felt into a manageable sized parcel. Place this folded parcel on the bubble side of the felting mat.

19 Unfold the wet felt and lay the base fabric against the bubbles. If the felt is dry then sprinkle with cool soapy water.

20 Place your hands on the surface of the felt and gently manipulate with a light pressure, moving the felt against the rough bubbles, using the surface like an old-fashioned washboard. The manipulation 'fulls' the felt in a rapid shrinkage process and the bubbles act to massage the wool fibers and pull them through the open weave of the fabric.

21 Very quickly you will see the felt wrinkling and shrinking before your eyes. Continue with this process until you have achieved the desired shrinkage and density. Stop when the felt appears firmer and the wrinkling is fairly even.

22 Rinse the felt with a solution of vinegar and water (half a cup of vinegar to a bucket of water) to remove the soap.

23 To finish the piece, press and lay flat to dry.

21

wrap skirt

This garment can be used as either a skirt or a wrap – it's always useful to have multi-purpose items in your wardrobe. Wear over leggings, pants or as an overskirt, and find a nice pin to attach it at the hip.

wrap skirt

MATERIALS Merino wool tops, silk tops and a base fabric of tissue silk, (silk gauze) in the skirt shown, all in 'Walnut' from Spiral Dyed.
QUANTITY 1½ oz of wool in total.
LAID-OUT SIZE 86" x 39". FINISHED SIZE 56½ x 27½".

2

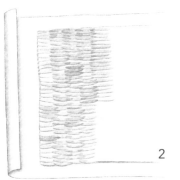

2

Laying out

1 Lay the tissue silk on the smooth side of your felting mat and use masking tape to hold in place.

2 Gently pull a manageable length off the wool tops, then tease the wool apart in small tufts and lay on top of the silk fabric in your chosen pattern. I have used one layer in even rows like roof tiles to show the rainbow-dyed wool tops to best effect.

3 If you want a heavier coverage of wool, lay out a second light layer at right angles to the first layer or at random.

4 Decorate the surface by laying silk tops evenly across the surface.

5 Remove the masking tape and cover the laid-out fleece with netting.

Wetting down the fleece

6 Fill a plastic bottle that has holes in the lid with cool water and detergent – with nuno felt you need a more soapy mixture to make the wool adhere to the base fabric. Carefully shake a small amount of this mixture onto the laid-out fleece.

7 With your hand inside a plastic bag, rub the lightly wetted fleece very gently in a circular motion. Work from the middle to the edges to avoid moving the pieces around. *Work very slowly and gently* – you do not want to disturb what you've just worked so hard to lay out. Continue until the entire piece is flat and moist, but not too wet – *dry areas will not felt.*

8 Very gently remove the net, lifting carefully at the corners and gently pulling away the wool that catches (it will catch because it starts to felt to the net if you rub too vigorously).

9 Lay a sheet of fine plastic over your work and press it gently into place as if you are laminating the wool and silk between the plastic and the felting mat.

10 Roll the fleece up in the felting mat and place rubber bands around the ends of the roll to keep it secure.

Rolling the felt

Nuno felt takes more rolling than normal flat felt as there are less wool fibers to tangle and mat together.

11 Lay a folded towel on the table and place the rolled felting mat on top of it – this is to soak up the drips and to stop the felting mat from slipping as you roll.

12 Roll the felting mat forward and backward 100 times, then unroll and check that your work hasn't moved (it's unlikely to have done so if covered with a sheet of plastic).

13 Gently reposition any pieces that have moved, then re-roll the felting mat from the opposite direction. Repeat the rolling and checking process three more times, rolling 100 times each time, and re-rolling from the opposite end each time.

14 Now repeat the rolling and checking process four more times, re-rolling from the opposite direction each time, and rolling 200 times each time. Check and reposition any pieces that may have moved between each turn.

15 Unroll and carefully lift a corner of the plastic. Lift the silk very gently and check the back to see if the wool fibers have evenly penetrated the surface. If so, continue to the fulling stage. If not, continue rolling until the wool fibers evenly penetrate the fabric.

Fulling the felt

16 Gently fold the wet felt into a manageable sized parcel. Place this folded parcel on the bubble side of the felting mat.

17 Unfold the wet felt and lay the base fabric against the bubbles. If the felt is dry then sprinkle with cool soapy water.

18 Place your hands on the surface of the felt and gently manipulate with a light pressure, moving the felt against the rough bubbles, using the surface like an old-fashioned washboard. The manipulation 'fulls' the felt in a rapid shrinkage process and the bubbles act to massage the wool fibers through the open weave of the fabric.

19 Very quickly you will see the felt wrinkling and shrinking before your eyes. Continue with this process until you have achieved the desired shrinkage and density. Stop when the felt appears firmer and the wrinkling is fairly even.

20 Rinse the felt with a solution of vinegar and water (half a cup of vinegar to a bucket of water) to remove the soap.

21 To finish the piece, press and lay flat to dry.

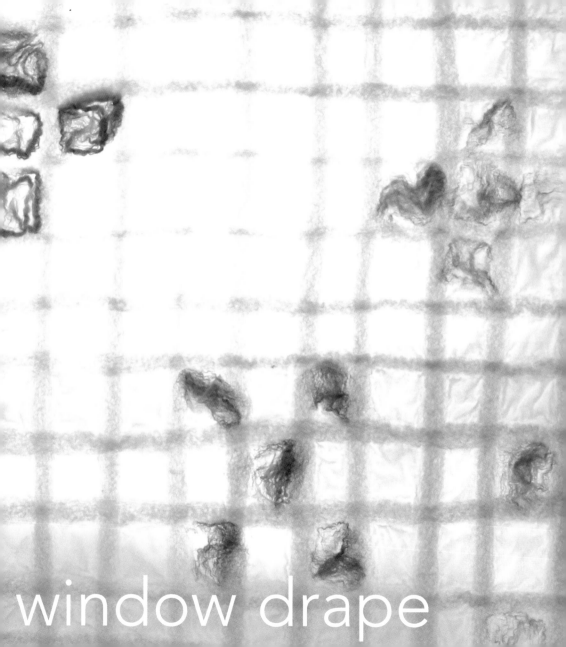

window drape

The beauty of this technique – sandwiching felt between other fabrics – is that it can be used to create versatile items. This window drape would be equally lovely as an evening wrap, overskirt or bed cover. Or make smaller pieces to use as placemats or a table runner. I like it as a window covering as I enjoy the play of light through the wool and silk.

window drape

MATERIALS Merino wool tops, shown in natural from First Editions Fibers & Yarns, silk tops dyed in 'Waterlily' from Spiral Dyed, and the base fabric is a double layer of tissue silk (silk gauze) from The Silk Company, measuring 172" x 39" in total. The wool and silk tops are sandwiched in a grid design between two layers of silk gauze.

QUANTITY 1½ oz of wool in total.

LAID-OUT SIZE 86" x 39". FINISHED SIZE 73½" x 33".

Laying out

1 Lay the first piece of tissue silk (86" x 39") on the smooth side of your felting mat and use masking tape to hold it in place.

2 Unroll a length of wool tops that is slightly longer than the silk (this project used 94" vertical strips).

3 Split the piece of wool tops into several fine slivers (8 to 12 pieces) and carefully lay these along the

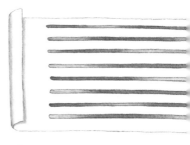

3

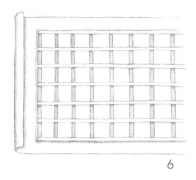

6

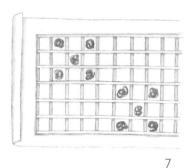

7

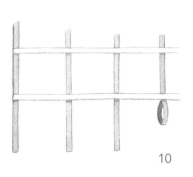

10

length of the silk in rows 1–2" apart, leaving some overhang at one end, to form a fringe at the bottom of the drape.

4 Continue until you have covered the tissue silk with rows of wool.

5 Unroll a length of wool tops that is slightly wider than the tissue silk. Split this length several times to make the pieces the same width as the vertical strips.

6 Working from edge to edge, lay these slivers across the silk in columns from top to bottom, to form a grid pattern.

7 Now pull fine tufts from the silk tops and place these inside some of the squares in a random pattern – don't fill all the spaces or the light won't shine through the curtain.

8 Carefully cover the laid-out design with the second piece of tissue silk.

9 With the second layer of silk in place, trim away the excess wool that is protruding from both sides and the top – don't cut the bottom overhang.

10 The wool overhanging along the bottom should be trimmed so that it is even, and then folded in half and tucked under the top layer of silk so it becomes a fringe.

11 Remove the masking tape and cover the laid-out fleece with netting.

Wetting down the fleece

12 Fill a plastic bottle that has holes in the lid with cool water and detergent – with nuno felt you need a more soapy mixture to make the wool adhere to the base fabric. Shake a small amount of this mixture onto the laid-out fleece.

13 With your hand inside a plastic bag, rub the lightly wetted fleece very gently in a circular motion. Work from the middle to the edges to avoid moving the pieces around. *Work very slowly*

and gently. Continue until the entire piece is flat and moist, but not too wet – *dry areas will not felt.*

14 Very gently remove the net, lifting carefully at the corners and gently pulling away the wool that catches (it will catch because it starts to felt the net if you rub too vigorously).

15 Lay a sheet of fine plastic over your work and press it gently into place as if you are laminating the wool and silk between the plastic and the felting mat.

16 Roll the piece up in the felting mat and place rubber bands around the ends of the roll to keep it secure.

Rolling the felt

Nuno felt takes more rolling than normal flat felt as there are fewer wool fibers to tangle and mat together.

17 Lay a folded towel on the table and place the rolled felting mat on top of it – this is to soak up the drips and to stop the felting mat from slipping as you roll.

18 Roll the felting mat forward and backward 100 times, then unroll and check that your work hasn't moved (it's unlikely to have done so if covered with a sheet of plastic).

19 Gently reposition any pieces that have moved, then re-roll the felting mat from the opposite direction. Repeat the rolling and checking process three more times, rolling 100 times each time, and re-rolling from the opposite end each time.

20 Now repeat the rolling and checking process four more times, re-rolling from the opposite direction each time and rolling 200 times each time.

21 Unroll and carefully lift a corner of the plastic. Lift the silk very gently and check the back to see if the wool fibers are evenly penetrating the surface. If so, continue to the fulling stage. If not, continue rolling until the wool fibers evenly penetrate the fabric.

Fulling the felt

22 Unroll then gently fold the wet felt into a manageable sized parcel. Place this folded parcel on the bubble side of the felting mat.

23 Unfold the wet felt with the base fabric against the bubbles. If the felt is dry then sprinkle with cool soapy water.

24 Place your hands on the surface of the felt and gently manipulate with a light pressure, moving the felt against the rough bubbles, using the surface like an old-fashioned washboard. The manipulation 'fulls' the felt in a rapid shrinkage process and the bubbles act to massage the wool fibers through the open weave of the fabric.

25 Very quickly you will see the felt wrinkling and shrinking before your eyes. Continue with this process until you have achieved the desired shrinkage and density. Stop when the felt appears firmer and the wrinkling is fairly even.

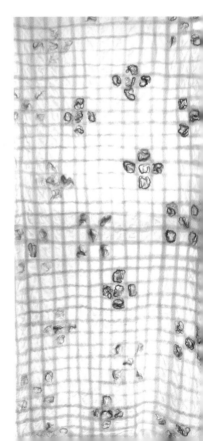

26 Rinse the felt with a solution of vinegar and water (half a cup of vinegar to a bucket of water) to remove the soap.

27 To finish the piece, press and lay flat to dry.

Here are some ideas for making flat felt pieces which do not use traditional methods of laying out. As long as the wool fibers cross at some points they will felt together. It then becomes a question of strength and whether the technique is suitable for the purpose you have in mind.

Once again these techniques can be used to create a variety of different projects or to embellish other pieces. For instance, the edges of the grid curtain would make great fringing on a scarf. Small spiral rolls, like those in the placemat project, were used for the treetops in the picture project.

new
techniques

placemats
& coasters

These placemats and coasters have been made using two designs that are a variation on a theme. By laying out rainbow- or spiral-dyed wool tops you will have variations in color that really make these designs work. Split the wool tops into fine slivers and wind them into whatever size spiral that you like. You can either create one large spiral for each placemat, or build it up using small spirals. Mix these designs up or make matching sets. The beauty of these little placemats comes from using rainbow-dyed wool tops. If these are not available lay two or three colors side by side and spiral them together.

placemats & coasters

MATERIALS Merino wool tops shown here from Spiral Dyed in 'antique rose'.

QUANTITY The large placemats use approximately ½ oz.

The small coasters use approximately ⅛ oz.

LAID-OUT SIZE 12" for the placemats, 5" for the coasters.

FINISHED SIZE 10" placemats, 4" coasters.

Laying out

1 Work on the smooth side of your felting mat and make several placemats and coasters at a time.

2 Break off a length of wool tops and split this piece into 6–8 lengths. Lay these lengths in a spiral on the bubble wrap until you have reached the size you want; the placemats pictured measure 12" across and the coasters 5".

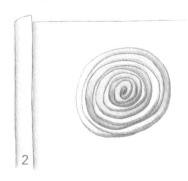

3

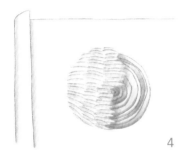

4

3 For an alternative design, make several small spiral rolls and lay them beside each other like petals on a flower.

4 Cover these shapes with a layer of wool tops laid out like roof tiles, curving at the edges so there are no bits of wool sticking out (if there are any they can be trimmed off before you full the mat).

5 When finished, cover the laid-out fleece with netting.

Wetting down the fleece

6 Fill a plastic bottle that has holes in the lid with warm water and a few drops of detergent. Carefully shake this mixture over your work to wet down the fleece.

7 With your hand inside a plastic bag, rub the wetted area gently in a circular motion. Work from the middle towards the edges to avoid moving the pieces around. *Work very slowly –* you do not want to disturb what you've just laid out. Continue until the entire piece is flat and wet but not dripping – *dry areas will not felt.*

8 Very gently remove the net, lifting carefully at the corners and gently pulling away the wool that catches (it will catch because it starts to felt to the net if you rub too vigorously).

9 To keep areas of detail undisturbed while rolling, lay a fine plastic drop sheet over your work, and gently press the plastic into place.

10 Roll the piece up in the felting mat and place rubber bands around the ends of the roll to keep it secure.

Rolling the felt

11 Lay a folded towel on the table and place the rolled felting mat on top of it – this is to soak up the drips and to stop the felting mat from slipping as you roll.

12 Roll the felting mat forward and backward 50 times, unroll and check that the work hasn't moved (it's unlikely to have done so if covered with a sheet of plastic).

13 Gently reposition any pieces that have moved, turn the felt ninety degrees then re-roll the felting mat. Repeat the rolling and checking process three more times, turning the felt ninety degrees between turns and rolling 50 times each time.

14 Repeat the rolling and checking process four more times, turning the work ninety degrees between turns and rolling 200 times each time.

15 Unroll and gently fold the wool into a small parcel and squeeze out the water.

16 Reheat the felt by dipping it in hot water and squeezing out the excess.

17 Unfold the felt, reposition it on the felting mat, and roll up quickly to retain the heat.

18 Roll another 200 times, unroll and check. Repeat twice, turning the felt ninety degrees each time. You will see the wool starting to shrink up and go bubbly and lumpy like pebbles – this is good, it's what we want.

Fulling the felt

Work on each mat or coaster individually during these steps and pull into shape as you go.

19 Fold the wet felt into a small parcel and squeeze out all the water.

20 Throw this parcel with all your might against a towel on your work table or on the floor. Refold it when it comes undone and repeat this throwing process about 20 times – you will see the felt begin to shrink rapidly.

21 Turn the felting mat to bubble side up. Unfold the wet felt and reposition it on the mat surface. If the felt is dry then re-sprinkle with warm soapy water.

22 Place your hands on the surface of the felt and gently manipulate it with a light pressure, moving

the felt against the rough bubbles, using the surface like an old-fashioned washboard. This kneading process 'fulls' the felt causing rapid shrinkage as the bubbles act like a massager, gently moving the wool fibers against each other.

23 Continue to heat and manipulate the felt either by rolling or kneading until you have achieved the desired shrinkage and density.

24 To strengthen the edges of the felt roll them under your hand against the bubbles of the felting mat.

25 Rinse the felt with a solution of vinegar and water (half a cup of vinegar to a bucket of water) to remove the soap.

26 To finish the piece, press and lay flat to dry, finishing with a steam iron on wool setting when partly dry for a lovely smooth finish.

grid curtain

This design can be used as suggested, or a fringe can be added at both ends to make a very dramatic scarf. This piece uses a small amount of wool, so it won't shrink too much.

grid curtain

MATERIALS Merino wool tops, shown in pink rainbow-dyed from Yarn Barn.
QUANTITY 2¾ oz of wool in total.
LAID-OUT SIZE 82" x 39". FINISHED SIZE 66" x 31".

Laying out

1 Work on the smooth side of your felting mat.

2 Unroll the wool tops and break off the required length for your curtain (allowing for shrinkage). The curtain shown uses lengths of 82".

3 Split the wool tops into 6–8 fine slivers and carefully lay these on the pool cover in rows about 2" apart, working from edge to edge until you reach the width you want. The curtain pictured was laid out to a width of 39".

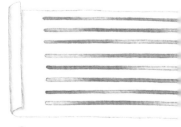

3

4 Unroll a 39" length of wool tops and split this length until it is the same width as the vertical strips you have just laid out.

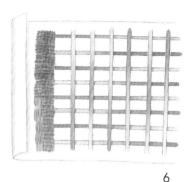

6

5 Lay these pieces across the wool rows in columns from top to bottom at regular intervals, also working from edge to edge – allow some overhang to make a fringe along the side.

6 Across the top edge of the curtain lay out two or three layers at right angles to each other, to cover the top edges of the rows of wool tops – this will form the top of your curtain.

7 Cover the laid-out fleece with netting.

Wetting down the fleece

8 Fill a plastic bottle that has holes in the lid with warm water and a few drops of detergent. Carefully shake this mixture over your work to wet down the fleece.

9 With your hand inside a plastic bag, rub the wetted area very gently in a circular motion. Work from the middle towards the edges to avoid moving the pieces around. *Work very slowly and gently* – you do not want to disturb what you've just laid out. Continue until the entire piece is flat and wet but not dripping – *dry areas will not felt.*

10 Very gently remove the net, lifting carefully at the corners and gently pulling away the wool that catches (it will catch because it starts to felt to the net if you rub too vigorously).

11 Protect the wool by laying a sheet of fine plastic over the top before rolling up in the felting mat.

12 Roll the piece up in the felting mat and place rubber bands around the ends of the roll to keep it secure.

Rolling the felt

13 Lay a folded towel on the table and place the rolled felting mat on top of it – this is to soak up the drips and to stop the felting mat from slipping as you roll.

14 Roll the felting mat forward and backward 50 times, unroll and check that the work hasn't moved (it's unlikely to have done so if covered with a sheet of plastic).

15 Gently reposition any pieces that have moved, then re-roll the felting mat from the opposite direction. Repeat the rolling and checking process three more times, turning the felt ninety degrees between turns, re-rolling the felting mat from the opposite direction each time and rolling 50 times each time.

16 Repeat the rolling and checking process four more times. Re-roll the felting mat from the opposite direction each time and roll 200 times each time.

17 Unroll and gently fold the wool into a small parcel and squeeze out the water.

18 Reheat the felt by dipping it in hot water and squeezing out the excess.

19 Unfold the felt, reposition it on the felting mat, and roll up quickly to retain the heat.

20 Roll another 200 times, unroll and check. Repeat twice, re-rolling from the opposite end of the felting mat each time. You will see the wool starting to shrink up and go bubbly and lumpy like pebbles – this is good, it's what we want.

Fulling the felt

21 Unroll then gently fold the wet felt into a manageable sized parcel. Place this folded parcel on the felting mat with the bubble side up. If the felt is dry then sprinkle it with cool soapy water.

22 Place your hands on the surface of the felt and gently manipulate with a light pressure, moving the felt against the rough bubbles, using the surface like an old-fashioned washboard. The manipulation 'fulls' the felt in a rapid shrinkage process and the bubbles act to massage the wool fibers.

23 To harden the strips of felt, roll the whole curtain into a big sausage and roll backward and forward, unrolling often to check that the curtain is not felting to itself. Rub the fringe in your hands so that it forms points and sits well. Stretch into shape.

24 Rinse the felt with a solution of vinegar and water (half a cup of vinegar to a bucket of water) to remove the soap.

25 To finish the piece, press and lay flat to dry.

templates

Templates for the scarf with flowers (page 59)
Template shapes are at 50%. Photocopy at 200% to obtain correct size.

Template for the decorative flags (page 71)
Template shape is at 50%. Photocopy at 200% to obtain correct size.

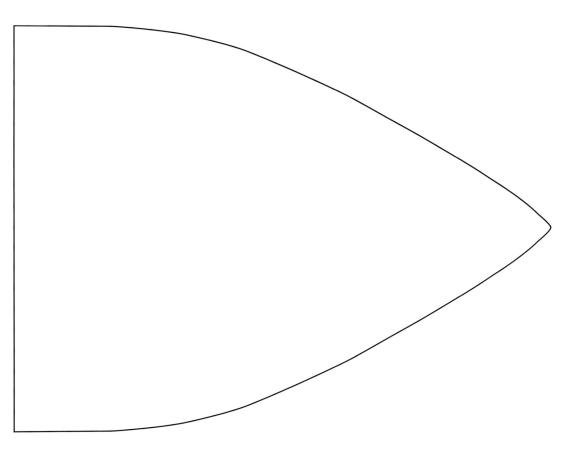

glossary

BATT
Layered carded wool or sheet of wool, which has been prepared for felting.

CARDING
A process where the fibers are opened up and aligned, and foreign matter removed.

CRIMP
The natural kink along the length of the wool fiber.

FELT
A pressed matted fabric formed by heat, moisture and friction.

FELTING
The whole process from fleece to fabric, and can also refer to the first part of the process when the wool is wet down and carefully rolled into a soft, loose fabric.

FLEECE
The shorn wool of a sheep. It can mean the whole fleece or just a mass of fibers.

FULLING
The final step of the felting process. During this process the soft fabric is rolled, then rubbed and pounded vigorously to make it shrink and compact, becoming a firm felt. This is an essential process and helps prevent pilling.

MICRON
A unit of measure of wool-fiber diameter, equal to a millionth of a meter.

NOIL
A short fiber combed from fleece during preparation, and used for surface embellishment.

NOPS

Pieces of silk or wool that are left over after the carding process.

NUNO FELT

Felting onto a layer of fabric.

PRE-FELT

Describes the stage at which the felting process has just begun; the fibers are beginning to matt together, but have not yet begun to shrink. Also known as half-felt.

ROVING AND PENCIL ROVING

Slivers of fiber similar to tops, but prepared in long narrow strips – available by the yard or by the ball.

SLIVER

A continuous rope of loose unspun wool fibers, which have been carded and combed.

WOOL TOP

A continuous rope of loose unspun wool fibers, which have been carded and combed.

felting tips

- Don't throw any of your failed experiments away – they can always be cut up and used for pre-felt projects.

- Is it felted yet? Time for the pinch test: if the two layers can be pulled apart then it is not felted – heat it up and give it another 200 rolls, then test again.

- Wetting down wool batts requires more water than wool tops, as there is a greater density of wool to soak through.

- To make very smooth felt: work with cool water; do not reheat; roll more and throw and manipulate by hand less. This slows down the fulling process, resulting in a smoother finish.

- Use the *tips* of the fingers to pull out tufts of wool for laying out.

- Do not hold the fleece too near the end from which you are pulling or you will not be able to pull it off the wool tops.

- Too much soap can prevent the wool from entangling – it creates slippage instead.

- Create a fringe with knitting yarn by allowing some to hang over the edge of the laid-out wool tops.

- Light and feathery edges on your felt might look pretty, but they are not very strong and may tear.

- A piece of felt that is to be decorative can be softly felted, while one that is going to be used often needs to be thoroughly fulled.

- When space is as at a minimum and you need to lay out something that's very long, try laying out a small section at a time, wetting it down, then rolling up the felting mat and continuing until you reach your desired length.

- Use a contrasting colored thread to stitch pre-felts so you can easily find the thread to pull it out.

- Pull your felt into shape before it's dry so that it's as even as possible.

- When making nuno felt, use masking tape to secure the corners of the fabric to the felting mat so it doesn't move while being laid out. Remember to remove the tape once the design is laid out and before you wet down.

- If your work is too wet, drain off some of the water after you have rolled up the felting mat or mop gently with a towel.

- Whenever you make a piece, note how many layers you have used and how much shrinkage has occurred. These are important factors in replicating a piece of felt. It is a good idea to record your discoveries with each fiber you experiment with.

felt resources

Further reading

Most of these feltmaking books and journals are currently available through bookshops or online. If unavailable or out of print, try to find them though libraries or feltmaking organizations. Don't be limited to felt books – look for titles on textiles and design, embroidery, machine embroidery and beading for inspiration.

The Art of Feltmaking, Anne Einset Vickrey, Watson-Guptill Publications, USA, 1997.

The Art of the Feltmaker, Mary E. Burkett, Abbott Hall Art Gallery, England, 1979.

Echoes, quarterly publication from The International Feltmakers Association.

Exploring Feltmaking, Joan Fisher, Kangaroo Press, Sydney, 1997.

'The Fabric of History', *National Geographic*, Vol. 173, No. 5 May 1988, p.p. 552–591.

Feltmaking, Deborah McGavock & Christine Lewis, Crowood Press, England, 2000.

Feltmaking: Fabulous Wearables, Jewelry & Home Accents, Chad Alice Hagen, Lark Books, USA, 2002.

Feltmaking: Techniques and Projects, Inge Evers, Lark Books, USA, 1987.

Feltwork, Victoria Brown, Lorenz Books, England, 1996.

Fundamentals of Felt Making – Scandinavian-style Felting, Patricia Sparks, Shuttle Craft Books, USA, 1992.

How to Make Felt, Anne Belgrave, Search Press, England, 1995.

New Directions for Felt, an Ancient Craft, Gunilla Paetau Sjoberg, Interweave Press, USA, 1996.

Traditional Textiles of Central Asia, Janet Harvey, Thames & Hudson, London/New York, 1997.

Feltmaking associations, classes & tutors

The best way to find felt classes is through feltmaking associations, textile groups, hand spinners and weavers, art and craft suppliers and independent felt tutors. If there are no groups listed in your area, contact the International Feltmakers Association in the UK, or try searching online.

USA

Handweavers Guild of America, Inc.
1255 Buford Highway, Suite
SUWANEE
Georgia 30024
p 678 730 0010
hga@weavespindye.org
www.weavespindye.org

North American Felters Network
1032 SW Washington Street
ALBANY
Oregon 97321
www.peak.org/~sparkfeltmakers.html

Columbia Weavers & Spinners' Guild
PO Box 124
COLUMBIA
MO 65205
http://cwsg.missouri.org

Northeast Feltmakers Guild
www.NeFeltMakersGuild.org

Northeast Handspinners Association
www.northeasthandspinners.org

Bonnie Ahrens
ABC Ranch
Felt classes have included traditional Turkish felting.
15249 Highway 19
MARTINSBURG
MISSOURI 65264
p 573 492 6472
www.abcranch.com

John C. Cambell Folk School
Short courses in traditional arts and crafts
BRASSTOWN
North Carolina 28765-0037
p 1 800 365 5724
www.folkschool.org

Chasing Rainbows Dye Works
Nancy Finn
Classes in color, hand-dying of silks
and fibers
1700 Hilltop Drive
WILLETS
California 95490
Nancy. finn@sbc.global.net

Jill Gully
Outback Fibers
Workshops and private classes.
312 Oak Plaza Cove
GEORGETOWN
Texas 78628
p 800 276 5015
www.outbackfibers.com

Penland School of Crafts
Post Office Box 37
PENLAND
North Carolina 28765-0037
p 828 765 2359
www.penland.org

Patricia Spark
Workshops, courses, and resourses
1032 SW Washington Street
ALBANY
Oregon 97321
spark@peak.org
www.sparkfiberarts.com

Wild Turkey Feltmakers
Polly Stirling (inventor of Nuno Felt)
and colleagues travel across North
America to provide a variety of
lessons and workshops.
www.wildturkeyfeltmakers.com

AUSTRALIA
TAFTA
(The Australian Forum for Textile Arts)
PO BOX 38
THE GAP
Qld 4061
p +61 (7) 3300 6491
f +61 (9) 3300 2148
tafta@iinet.net.au
www.ggcreations.com.au/tafta/

Felt Good Workshops
Felt classes for beginners to advanced.
Demonstrations, speaking engagements
and consulting. Commissions welcome.
Robyn Steel-Stickland
MELBOURNE
p +61 (3) 9885 6440
robyn@creativewomen.com.au
www.creativewomen.com.au/feltgood

NEW ZEALAND

Auckland Fun Felters
c/o Patricia Hagen
AUCKLAND
p +64 9 5280 322
pated@actrix.co.nz

New Zealand Felters Newsletter
c/o Pam & Dave Robinson
196 Tukapa Street
New Plymouth 4601

SOUTH AFRICA

The Midlands Arts & Crafts
Society Felters
DURBAN
South African Art Information Directory
info@saaid.co.za

UK & EUROPE

International Feltmakers Association
www.feltmakers.com

Websites

www.feltmakers.com

www.nuno.com

www.textilearts.net

www.weavespindye.org

www.filtmaker.no

www.knitty.com

www.grima.dk

www.werkraumtextil.de

www.chadalicehagen.com

www.feltmaker.co.uk

www.sarah-lawrence.com

www.northwestweavers.org

http://www.creativefibre.org.nz/org/north.htm

Places to see felt

Felt is appearing in more venues every week: art and textile galleries and museums; interior design stores; and designer fashion and accessory boutiques. Also look in the latest fashion and interiors magazines.

The Textile Museum
2320 "S" Street NW
WASHINGTON, DC
p 202 667 0441
www.textilemuseum.org

Textile Museum of Canada
55 Centre Avenue
TORONTO
Ontario M5G 2H5
info@textile
feltworks@bigpond.com

Kent State University Museum
P.O. Box 5190
Rockwell Hall
KENT, Ohio 44242-0001
p 330 672 3450
www.dept.kent.edu/museum

American Textile History Museum
491 Dutton Street
LOWELL
Massachusetts 01854
p 978 441 0400
www.athm.org

The Goldstein Museum of Design
University of Minnesota
240 McNeal Hall
1985 Bufford Avenue
ST. PAUL
Minnesota 55108
p 612 624 7434
http://goldstein.che.umn.edu

Nordic Heritage Museum
3014 NW 67th Street
SEATTLE
Washington 98117
p 206 789 5707
www.nordicmuseum.org

Society of Contemporary Craft
2100 Smallman Street
PITTSBURGH
Pennsylvania 15222
www.contemporarycraft.org

Quixotic Market Place
501 Chapala Street, Suite E
SANTA BARBARA
California 93101
p 805 568 1918
www.quixoticcreations.com

Tamarack Gallery
One Tamarack Park
BECKLEY
West Virginia 25801
www.tamarackwv.com

Massachusetts Sheep and Woolcraft Fair
www.masheepwool.org

Michigan Fiber festival, Inc.
P.O. Box 744
HASTINGS, MI 49058
www.michiganfiberfestival.org

New York and Wool Festival
Dutchess County Sheep and Wool Growers
RHINEBECK, NY
www.sheepandwool.com

Vermont Sheep and Wool Festival
Champion Valley Exposition
ESSEX JUNCTION, VT
www.vermontsheep.org

Australian Sheep and Wool Show
(Bendigo, Victoria)
This is the most important wool event
in Australia, held in July each year at
the Bendigo Showgrounds. You'll find
competitions, exhibitions, demonstrations,
fashion parades and felting supplies.
For details of the woolcraft section:
p +61 (3) 5443 8965
mgrylls@netcon.net.au

The Hermitage Museum in St Petersburg,
Russia
2 Dvortsovaya Square
190000
p +812 571 3420
visitorservices@hermitage.ru

Suppliers

This is not an exhaustive list of suppliers, but includes those mentioned in this book. Don't despair if there isn't a supplier close to you. Most have websites and mail-order services.

USA

Crown Mountain Farms
Fiber, dyes, buttons, classes
VELM
Washington
p 360 894 1738
www.crownmountainfarms.com

Fascinations Fiber Gallery & Studio
Merino roving; silk slivers, silk tops and special blends
211 Bannister, Suite 9A
PLAINWELL
Michigan 49080-9353
p 269 685 7077
www.hookedonfelt.com

Marr Haven Wool Farm
Premium wool and related products for felters
722 39th Street
ALLEGAN
Michigan 49010-9353
p 269 673 8800
www.marrhaven.com

Morehouse Farm
Sheeps Clothing
2 Rock City Road
MILIAN
NY 12571
p 1 845 758 3710
www.morehousefarm.com

The Needle Lady
Mimi Hyde
Fine fibers and felting tools
114 E. Main Street
CHARLOTTESVILLE
Virginia 22903
p 434 296 4625
www.needlelady.com

The Spinsters Treadle
Pool covers in custom sizes, felting soap and fiber
1640 Tyrone Road
MORGANTOWN
West Virginia 26508
p 304 284 0774
www.spinsterstreadle.com

Outback Fibers from
the Wool Shed
312 Oak Plaza
GEORGETOWN
Texas 78628
p 800 276 5015
www.outbackfibers.com

Paradise Fibers
Handpainted yarn and roving
3353 East Trent Avenue
SPOKANE, WA 99202
p 509 599 6986
p 888 320 SPIN (7746)
www.paradisefibers.com

Wooly Comforts
Premium wool roving and related items
Box 2038
CHILLICOTHE
Ohio 45601
p 740 775 1916
www.woolycomforts.com

CANADA

Sun Bench Fibres
#1-8979 Broadway Street
CHILLIWACK
BC, V2P 5V9
p 604 793 0058
p Toll-free (North America) 866 793 0058
www.sunbenchfibres.com

The Yarn Source
2661 Highway 62 south
RR1, BLOOMFIELD
Ontario K0K 1G0
p 613 393 2899
www.yarnsource.ca

AUSTRALIA

Felt Good
Pool covers for use as felting mats,
wool tops and felting tables.
Robyn Steel-Stickland
104 Albion Road
ASHBURTON
VIC 3147
p +61 (3) 9885 6440
robyn@creativewomen.com.au
www.creativewomen.com.au/feltgood

First Edition Fibres & Yarn
Large range of natural and solid colors.
Merino and non-Merino/silk. Pure exotic
fibers including tussah silk and angora
rabbit.
Lot 6 Charles Street
EUROA
VIC 3866
p +61 (3) 5795 3578
f +61 (3) 5795 3578

Margaret Peel's Fiber Supplies
Silk yarns, carded mohair, wool, alpaca,
de-haired cashmere and rabbit.
PO BOX 94
WERRIS CREEK
NSW 2341
p +61 (2) 6744 5214
peel6@bigpond.com
www.margaret-peel.com.au

Spiral Dyed Fibers & Threads
Jacinta Leishman
38 Hawkes Road
WARRANDYTE
VIC 3113
p +61 (3) 9844 4104
Jacinta@spiraldyed.com
www.spiraldyed.com

The Silk Company
Tissue silk supplies.
PO Box 286
BURNSIDE
SA 5066
p +61 (8) 8379 9064

Treetops Colour Harmonies
Nancy Ballesteros
Fine Merino tops, tussah silk tops, bombyx
silk tops, silk throwsters waste and silk laps.
Available in hand-dyed repeatable colour
harmonies and solids.
6 Benwee Road
FLOREAT
WA 6014
p +61 (8) 9387 3007
f +61 (8) 9387 1747
nancy@treetopscolours.com.au
www.treetopscolours.com.au

Yarn Barn
Carded Merino slivers, yarn, in a variety
of plys, rug wool and specialty yarns.
200 Reynard Street
COBURG
VIC 3058
p +61 (3) 9386 0361
www.yarnbarn.com

NEW ZEALAND
Ashford Handicrafts Ltd
Felting and craft materials and equipment.
Box 474
ASHBURTON
NEW ZEALAND
p +64 (3) 308 9087
f +64 (3) 308 9087
sales@ashford.co.nz

Shona Schofield Carding
1689 Tramway Road
1 R.D. Ashburton
NEW ZEALAND
p +64 3 303 9778
shonaschofield@xtra.co.nz
www.feltandfibre.co.nz

UK
The Handweavers Studio
29 Haroldstone Road
LONDON
E17 7AN
ENGLAND
p +44 20 8521 2281
www.handweaversstudio.co.uk

about the author

ROBYN STEEL-STICKLAND

My textile life started at school when I embroidered a pear on the pocket of my school apron. I love decorative sewing, but have avoided practical sewing ever since. I joined the Embroiderers' Guild of Victoria in my early 20s where I immersed myself in both traditional and contemporary embroidery techniques. In 1989 I enrolled in a Wearable Art course at the Canberra School of Art and had my introduction to feltmaking.

It wasn't until 1997 that my path led to a class with Jeanette Appleton from the UK, who taught me the art of making fine felt in a tidy manner with very little water, and showed me the endless possibilities offered by this ancient form of textile. Next I joined the Victorian Feltmakers Inc. and discovered a wonderful sharing group that welcomed and encouraged me. The most lasting influence has come from the tutors I have worked with, including Martine Van Zuilen, Molly Littlejohn, Jeanette Appleton and Beth Beede.

After years of attending workshops, entering my work in exhibitions and experimenting with various feltmaking techniques, I started to teach basic feltmaking classes for the Victorian Feltmakers Inc. I set up my business Felt Good, primarily to teach feltmaking, and secondly to promote and sell my work.

I get excited about color and pattern in my work, and I love working with wool. I love to see the build-up of a design and the possibilities of layering and building in stages that is so intrinsic to felt and collage. I get a big buzz from being part of the current trend in promoting feltmaking as an art form – to witness an ancient craft being reborn and to see the fabulous things that people are creating is very exciting. Working with adults and children who come up with new ideas and techniques to explore is also very rewarding.

contributing artists

ELIZABETH ARMSTRONG

Elizabeth is a practicing feltmaker and textile artist, who regularly runs stimulating workshops for beginner to advanced students. She is a proud advocate of Australian wool, and feels that we are lucky to have such a superb resource so readily available. Elizabeth has worked on several successful commissions and group exhibitions and is currently preparing for a solo exhibition.

KITTY CHUNG O'KANE

Kitty is a practicing artist who also runs a small business in art education. Kitty has lived in several countries in southeast Asia, and these experiences have had a lasting effect on her work and use of color. Felt has become a very important part of her teaching experience and her art, as it allows for the production of precise images using pre-felting techniques to create artwork with abstract qualities. Kitty has won major awards in the Fashion Fantasia competition in Tasmania, and has also won with entries in the Australian Fashion Designer of the Year awards.

CATHERINE O'LEARY

Catherine O'Leary is an inspiring designer and textile artist who has been making felt for 15 years. She loves the medium because it can be stitched and molded. Catherine is involved in many projects and continually experiments with new techniques. Her work has been featured in many textile publications and exhibitions, and her most recent project is her gallery 'Lumina' in Melbourne, which promotes the work of feltmakers from all over Australia.

acknowledgements

The following people are owed my sincere thanks. To my husband Gary and children, Julian and Tessa, who have put up with having no wife or mother for the duration of writing this book, and who have encouraged and supported me – without them, there would be no book. To Stacey for helping make felt, and for editing an early draft of the manuscript; to Kitty and Catherine for support, suggestions and advice; to Elizabeth for all of the above, plus nocturnal phone calls and emails, and turning up early on photo day to assist; to Rod for support, lending an ear, and for being fascinated by felt; to my sister Fleur for great encouragement and being a glamorous model; to Nonie for editing, encouraging and checking up on me; to Jacinta and Francesca for support; to family and friends who have encouraged me from the sidelines, looked after the children and checked up on me from time to time; and to Amber and Golly who kept me company, gave great creative input and left their mark. To my feltmaking and textile friends, especially members of the Victorian Feltmakers Inc. for working with me and sharing tips along the way; to my feltmaking students for asking questions and making me a better teacher; and to my generous and helpful new feltmaking friends.

On the publishing side: thanks to Jo Turner for asking me to write this book and take up one of the biggest challenges of my life; thanks to Julie Renouf for taking beautiful photographs, to Claire Tice for designing a gorgeous layout and Tim Clarke for fixing the words – together you've made it look quite scrumptious. And special thanks to Sue Carroll and Trina Carter of Montreux, 287 Wattletree Road, East Malvern, for generously allowing us to use your beautiful shop as a location and source of props, and to Lyn and Richard Amy for allowing us to take over your home for a photo session.